WHY I BELIEVE

WHY I BELIEVE

SENATOR JAKE GARN

ASPEN BOOKS
Salt Lake City, Utah

Why I Believe

Library of Congress Cataloging-in-Publication Data

    Garn, Jake.
        Why I believe / Jake Garn.
           p. cm.
        ISBN 1-56236-200-3 : $11.95
           1. Garn, Jake. 2. Mormons—Utah—Biography.
    3. Legislators—Utah—Biography. 4. Mormons—Utah—Religious
Life. 5. Legislators—Utah—Religious life. I. Title.
    BX8695.G33A3 1992
    289.3'092—dc20
    [B]   92-26486
                                         CIP

Printed in the United States of America

10 9 8 7 6 5 4 3 2

Cover design: Brian Bean
Cover Photo of Jake Garn: Michael Schoenfeld
Cover Photo of Space Shuttle Discovery: Courtesy Jake Garn

DEDICATION

This book is dedicated to my family, without whom my life would be meaningless.

To my parents Jacob Edwin Garn and Agnes Fern Christensen for giving me life itself and the great example to live it well.

To my sisters, Mildred Bingham and Janet Redenbaugh, for making it possible for me to reach adulthood.

To the mothers of my children, Hazel Rhae Thompson, as kind and gentle a person as ever lived, and to Kathleen Brewerton, who brought two families together as well as anyone possibly could. I will be eternally grateful to her.

To Jake, my oldest son, who overcame great obstacles to become a remarkable young man and father.

To Susan Horne, my daughter, who carries my kidney and is an example to all of us for her courage and faith.

To Ellen Reich, my daughter, who is talented and intelligent beyond my ability to describe.

To Jeff, my son, with all the personality anyone could hope for, and a great missionary in England.

To Brook Bingham, my stepson, who I am proud to call my own. He is soon to depart for the Australia Sydney Mission.

To Matthew Spencer, my fourth son, who is my friend and companion as I grow older.

To Jennifer, my beautiful, third daughter and seventh child, who does far more for my ego than being a United States Senator does.

And finally, to Kirsten, Spencer, Nathan, Allison, Hannah, Daniel, Ryan, Carlie, Lauren, and McKenzie, my grandchildren.

CONTENTS

ACKNOWLEDGEMENTS

Curtis Taylor is an outstanding young man and a talented writer. I would be very ungrateful if I did not extend my gratitude and thanks to him for untold hours working with me to put my thoughts and beliefs on paper. I find it very easy to express myself in verbal form but find it much more difficult in written form. Curtis made this transition possible. I also wish to thank Stan Zenk for his valuable help in proof-reading and editing.

MY FAMILY. Back row: Jeff Garn, Jake Garn, Sharon Garn, Nathan Garn, Lauren Reich, Todd Reich, Carlie Reich, Ellen Garn Reich, Matthew Garn, Allen Horne, Brook Bingham. *Front row:* Ryan Reich, Heidi Reich, McKenzie Garn, Jennifer Garn, Jake Garn, Spencer Garn, Kathleen Garn, Kirsten Garn, Daniel Horne, Susan Garn Horne, Allison Horne. *Not in picture:* Hannah Horne (deceased). (Photo

Introduction

One of the great blessings of my life in public service has been the opportunity of visiting with thousands of people. Besides meeting with dignitaries and leaders of the world—the so-called "elite"—I have also been blessed to meet many of the good, unheralded people who keep this world going. Many of these people have shared their dreams and visions of a better world with me, and I have grown because of it.

On occasion—perhaps too rarely—I have shared my dreams and visions with them—my testimony. On those rare, wonderful occasions, I have opened my heart and shared my belief that the world really can be better, that peace *can* break out, that suffering can be alleviated, and that love, that strongest of all balms, can permeate the world around us. With the Spirit sometimes touching me, I share the vision that God and prophets have shared with me that man really is divine, that with repentance and hard work he really can make his life noble and meaningful. When I share this testimony, I see again how true it is, and I am anxious to speed it along. I want to share this testimony with you.

But I want you to know *why* I have this testimony. I want you to know the reasons for my faith in God, for my belief in man, and for my love of this life. I want you to know why I believe.

. . . In The Family

On August 17, 1976, while working at my Salt Lake City office, I received a phone call from the Nebraska Highway Patrol. My secretary said that the patrolman wouldn't speak with her; he needed to speak with me for some reason. I took the phone and was told that most of my family—my wife, Hazel, and three of my children—had just been killed in an automobile accident. I put the phone down and everything began to blur.

I cannot describe what it is like to live with a wonderful woman for nineteen years, to have four beautiful children, then to be told that all but one of them are gone. I suddenly realized that without my family there was very little meaning in life. My family had always been paramount. It had come before all other responsibilities and concerns. It had been the source of my greatest joys and my greatest hopes. Now, with the exception of my oldest son, it was gone.

I went to my mother's home and found her and my son, Jake, there. I tried to give them the news. I began to sob uncontrollably as I embraced Jake and told him that we were the only ones left, that the rest of the family had been killed. My mother put her arms around me and tried to comfort me. I didn't hear her words at first. Suddenly the telephone rang. It was for me. The doctor at the hospital in Nebraska wanted to make sure that I understood the situation there and to verify the information my children were giving him. I thought I misheard him. As he continued, I cut in.

"You mean my children are there?" I asked. "Are they alive?"

"Oh, yes. They're fine. Miraculously, they were unhurt."

"But the highway patrolman told me that they had all been killed."

"No, no. He must have misunderstood. I'm sorry. The children are fine. When the car rolled, the roof caved in right above your wife's head, and her neck was broken. She was probably killed instantly. But the children are unhurt. They're fine. I'm very sorry for the mistake."

When I put the phone down I told Jake and my mother that the children were alive. A part of my life seemed to come back. But after a few minutes the weight and sadness returned. I couldn't do all that was expected of me now. I couldn't live without Hazel. I couldn't be a father and a mother to these children. I certainly couldn't be a senator anymore. As these feelings overwhelmed me, I began to cry again, my heart wanting to break, and my mother again comforted me.

"Jake," she said, "have I ever told you anything wrong in your life?"

"No," I answered.

"Then I'm not going to start now. I know that you hurt—we all do—but if you will follow the teachings of the Lord and live the way your father and I taught you, everything will be fine."

"No, Mother," I said, "everything won't be fine. It will never be fine again. In fact, I'm going back to Washington and resign from the Senate. And then I'm going to come back home and live here."

"Why?" she asked.

"Because I can't raise these kids alone. I need help from my family—from you and my sisters and the rest of the family. I can't cope with this alone."

"No, Jake, you can't do that."

"What?"

"You're not coming home."

"Yes, I am."

"No, you're not. I'll tell you what you're going to do. You're going back there and you're going to be the best senator you can for six months. Then, if at the end of six months, you still want to come home, I won't stop you; you can resign from the Senate and come home. But now is not the time to make that decision."

I looked at her, feeling her strength and her resolve, but I still didn't feel that she understood.

"And I'll promise you something else," she said. "You will marry again. And you'll have a wonderful companion, and you'll be happy. If you do what you've been taught all your life, you and your family will be all right."

"Mother, that makes me angry. I'm never getting married again. I don't *want* anybody else. I'm not getting married again under any circumstances."

"Yes, Jake, you will." She had her arm around me, and she patted my shoulder. "You'll remarry, and you'll be happy again."

I looked into her eyes and knew that she meant every word she was saying. She seemed to know that my future and my family's future would be far brighter than I could possibly believe then. She never once showed any emotions that would hurt me or cause me to lose resolve. While she comforted me she never shed a tear, though I know she cried afterwards. The most gentle woman I have ever known was suddenly a bedrock of strength. My mother gave me the hope I needed to make the right decisions and eventually find my way back to peace and happiness.

I *believe* in families. I believe that they are ordained of God and that they constitute our basic relationship—both here and in heaven. Everything that is really important in my life, everything that has led to accomplishment or joy, has come from the family. Along with my faith in God, it is the only thing that is worth all that I have, and it is the only thing that I can take with me back to God.

My sister Mildred's daughter, Leslie, and her husband, Jim, drove to Nebraska, picked up my children, and brought them to me in Denver. My other sister, Janet, and her husband took care of most of the arrangements for the funeral (something I doubt that I could have done), but I had to go to the funeral home for final arrangements and to see my wife for the last time. A very dear friend of mine, Dick Winder, offered to come along with me. This was very gracious of him as I was still feeling like I was living in a fog. I have never been a weak person emotionally, but when I walked up to the coffin and saw Hazel lying within its satin lining, I lost my strength. My knees went weak, and I started to fall. Fortunately, Dick was right there, and he grabbed me and put his arms around me. I don't know how long I stood there in his arms, but I'll never forget his act of kindness in literally supporting me as I offered my final good-byes to my wife of nineteen years.

I was dreading the trip back to Washington. We had been making our home there for nearly two years, and I couldn't stand the thought of going back there and finding everything the way it had been when we left for Utah earlier that summer. What I was most unprepared for was having to go through Hazel's things and put them away. I knew that going through her closets and handling her clothes would bring back memories—memories that I wasn't ready to face yet, and that her personal things, even the smell of her perfume, would only intensify the loneliness I already felt. The day came, though, when my children and I finally walked up to the door of our house for the first time since the accident. As we walked in, we were greeted by Dale and Elaine Ensign, two very dear friends of ours. They had called my secretary, who knew them well, and gotten the key to the house. Without us knowing, they had dusted, vacuumed, cleaned, brought flowers, and now had a full dinner waiting for us. There was no fanfare, no fuss; they just knew how difficult this would be. I thanked them for their kindness and invited them to join us for dinner. They declined and said that they would leave us to eat as a family. Before leaving, though, they said they would be by again soon to check on us and help in any way they could. These people are truly saints.

As we continued to receive love and support of many friends, I knew that the Lord was literally answering our prayers through them. When I needed companionship and support in the funeral home, he sent an angel, disguised as a lifelong friend, to stand beside me and lift me up. When our family needed a great act of service as we arrived in Washington, he sent two more angels, again looking just like dear friends, to offer their love and kindness. There is no way I can repay these debts or even show sufficient gratitude for them. I can only try to be available and willing when others need my help.

Other members of the family, too, came forward to help. Sue, our oldest daughter, sacrificed her desire to complete her last year of high school in Salt Lake and came back to Washington to help care for the smaller children. She filled the need well and basically became a second mother to them. The younger children were greatly blessed by this, and I know that Sue grew through the experience as well. I don't see how I can adequately repay her for this. My youngest daughter, Ellen, was only thirteen, but she was, and still is, a Daddy's girl and was a constant comfort to me during this terrible period.

In the next few months I found strength I didn't know I had. Following my mother's example, I made sure that I gave the children all the love and support I could. These were children, ranging from ten to eighteen years old, who had just lost the most important person in their lives. Although I, too, would go into my bedroom and cry at night, I tried to make sure that my children didn't see it. I had to be there to shoulder part of their burden, to relieve their pain as much as possible. The strength to do this came from three sources: the Lord, my mother, and good friends.

There were times when guilt crept in. I felt that if I had been there in the car, as we had originally planned, that the accident would never have happened. Hazel had fallen asleep at the wheel, causing the car to drift off the road, and I knew that if I had been along, even if I hadn't been driving, that such a situation probably wouldn't have come up; she wouldn't have been so tired. But even as these feelings came to me, a peaceful understanding also came that I couldn't blame myself for the accident. The loss of my wife and the loss of my children's mother was not my fault. The Lord didn't want any of us to carry this guilt. Although this feeling comforted me, it didn't last indefinitely and I had to return constantly to my Heavenly Father in prayer to regain the peace I needed.

There were times when my children needed more help than I could provide. Jeff, my youngest son at the time, suffered recurring nightmares. He had seen his mother lying lifeless on the ground after the accident. His dreams were filled with this scene night after night, and he often came and slept with me, which was good for both of us. I couldn't take his nightmares away, but I could pray for his peace, which eventually came. I know the Lord helped us in healing from these emotional scars as quickly as possible.

My mother remained a strong influence in our family, visiting us and talking to us on the phone often. Because my father had passed away by this time, it was important that we had her support.

Eventually we began receiving more negative reactions to the situation. I was amazed by the number of women who wrote to my office proposing marriage. In a very short period of time, literally hundreds of letters came in from all over the country, telling me that they knew that they were right for me, or that they were the mother my children needed. I was disgusted by the presumptuousness of these women, many of whom may have had sincere intentions but who honestly didn't seem to appreciate the grief we were experiencing. Cards and letters of condolence were greatly appreciated, but the letters of proposition were unfortunate and very uncalled-for. I eventually asked my chief legislative assistant, Joanne Neumann, to screen my letters and to make sure I didn't see these anymore.

Many friends, of course, suddenly had single women friends that I should meet. I was amazed at how everybody knew somebody that I should get to know. They were very well intentioned, but I just didn't have the slightest desire to meet other women at this time. I still felt a very strong attachment and loyalty to Hazel. Sometime that fall or winter, however, I did consent to meet one or two of these women, perhaps out of obligation to my friends, and I cannot adequately describe how uncomfortable I felt at these times. The problem was mine; even though Hazel had been gone for some time, I still felt that I was being unfaithful to her by going out to dinner with another woman. I found that these feelings of attachment take a long time to work through, at least longer than I had given them so far.

My feelings about remarriage had remained basically unchanged. Although I was willing to visit with other people, I still didn't have the slightest desire to find a new wife. Something else I also remembered of my feelings then was also confirmed: I couldn't be both father and mother to my children. Although Sue was doing a wonderful job in our home with the children, I knew that sometime she would want to pursue her own life and raise a family of her own. I also knew that my younger children would need a mother who was also my wife—a woman who would help us create a full family unit again.

As Christmas approached, I decided to take the children back to Utah for the holidays. I had done the shopping for my boys, but I needed help with the girls, so I called an old friend of mine, Kathleen Brewerton, and asked her if she could help me out. I had called her in the months before to give advice to me about raising the girls, and had even had her talk to my daughters on the phone once or twice. I had known her since I had been mayor of Salt Lake because her former husband was my administrative assistant. She had one son, Brook, who had always been a good friend of my son, Jeff. Of course she agreed to help me with the Christmas shopping as soon as we returned to Utah.

As it turned out, we spent more time together than I anticipated. Being a good friend of the family, she spent time at my mother's house and went shopping with me for the girls. As we spent this time together, I realized that I was comfortable with her. Perhaps because she had been a friend for so long, I didn't have the feelings of anxiety and newness that I had with other women. One night after Christmas, I asked her if she would go to dinner with me that Friday night. She looked at me and said, "Are you asking me for a date?" And I said, "Yes, I suppose I am."

I still wasn't cured completely of my fear of dating, however. I called another couple, Kim and Laurel Young, who were close friends of mine and Kathleen's, to double with us on this date. When I told Kathleen about the double date she laughed and said, "You don't dare go out with me alone, huh?" I told her that things had changed. Although I had spent many afternoons with her shopping and had known her for over five years, our relationship had suddenly changed; it had gone from a friendship situation to a dating situation, and I wanted to treat it differently. After the date when I took her home, she asked if I wanted to come in for a moment, and I said no. She asked me why not, and I said, "Well, I don't go into a girl's house on the first date. I never have, and I don't intend to start now." She laughed and said that she understood. The rules of the game had changed.

She came back to Washington for a week—bringing her sister with her—and we spent a wonderful time together. I would never say that I fell in love with her overnight, because I had known her for more than five years, but when it did happen, it happened quickly. My feelings began to change rapidly from not wanting to remarry to possibly considering it, to absolutely wanting it. I'm sure that this was a natural process, but I think that it was enhanced by the Lord when I had found the right woman for me and my family.

As Kathleen and I later discussed the idea of marriage, she raised questions that I couldn't answer. Because of her former marriage, for example, she was concerned about who her son would be sealed to, and of my being sealed to two women, and so forth. As a friend of ours, she had already heard of the standing joke between Hazel and me. It was joked that if polygamy ever came back, Hazel would always be my favorite. And Hazel would say, "No, I won't, because if polygamy ever comes back, I won't be there." Now Kathleen had to wonder if that was more than a joke. As she wrestled with these questions, we decided to seek another opinion, and this led to one of the most enjoyable and meaningful moments of our lives—a visit with President Kimball.

It was a few months after that Christmas when President Kimball graciously invited us into his office to discuss our concerns. We felt the Spirit the moment we walked in. His concern for us was evident, and humbling. After helping us feel at ease, he listened to our questions and tried to answer them. He said that he didn't have answers to all the questions in the gospel, however. He said that he too was still working out his salvation before the Lord and that he still had his tests and challenges. He said that he prayed to the Lord and often received answers, but that not everything had been revealed to him. Because of this, he said he did not know exactly how these relationships will be worked out, but he did know that through faithfulness all will be well and we will have much joy. I was touched by his honesty and humility. I absolutely knew that I could trust whatever he told us. Then we mentioned my first wife's attitude toward polygamy, and her reaction: "I won't be there." Kathleen told him that she was afraid of offending Hazel. President Kimball's demeanor seemed to change. From being somewhat hesitant in his earlier answers, he now became sure and spoke with firmness. He looked right at Kathleen and with a tear forming in his eye, he said, "I do know this: you have nothing to worry about. Not only will she accept you, she will put her arms around you and thank you for raising her children."

I will never forget that moment. All our fears left. All our questions, even the ones he hadn't completely answered, seemed to fade into insignificance. We both knew in that moment that we were doing the right thing. And so did he. Almost immediately following that, he wanted to know when we were getting married. We hesitated for a moment then I said that it probably wouldn't be for another six months to a year.

"Why not?" he asked.

"Well," I answered, "in my position, where everybody can see me, there might be a good deal of criticism. My wife has been dead for only nine months, and some might think it's too soon."

"You're right," he said. "Some will think it's too soon— mostly narrow-minded Mormons. I don't think you should wait."

I was surprised. "You don't think we should wait?"

"No. Brother Garn, if you hadn't had a good marriage, you wouldn't want to consider getting remarried yet. People who have unhappy marriages usually don't want to get remarried very rapidly. You were happy in your marriage, and I think you will be happy in this one. You may be aware that my mother passed away when I was a young boy, and my father remarried early, in less than a year—and I'm so grateful that he did. Your children need a mother, and Kathleen's boy needs a father. If you two love each other and you want to get married, you should not wait. The strength and love of a family are so much more important than any criticism you may receive."

I told him that we would think about it, and he said, "Well, that's the best advice I can give you, but let me ask, would you give me the privilege of marrying you?"

This was one thing I didn't have to think about. "Yes, President, we certainly would."

Of course, we took the Prophet's advice on everything. Before long we were calling his secretary, Arthur Haycock, to tell him that we had set April 8th as our wedding date and to ask if the President could marry us in the Manti Temple. He called back and said that he was very sorry, but that the President had important meetings that day in Salt Lake and couldn't possibly make it to Manti. I told him that was no problem, we would change our plans and be married in the Salt Lake Temple. Brother Haycock thought that would work out fine. President Kimball called me back a little later, though, and said that he didn't want us to change our plans just for him. He felt terrible for inconveniencing us. I assured him that it was no inconvenience to change our plans and be married in the Salt Lake

Temple. "If I have a choice of getting married in the temple I want or of being married by the Prophet," I said, "I'll take the Prophet every time."

"Well, Brother Garn," he said, "I certainly can do it quite easily in Salt Lake on the 8th."

"Then that's what we'll do."

"Are you sure? I know you wanted to get married in the Manti Temple."

"It's just not that important," I said. "We want to be married by you."

And I think I finally convinced him that he wasn't inconveniencing us too much. He is the most humble man I have ever known.

On the day of the wedding, our relatives and close friends were assembled, and President Kimball joined us at that special time in the sealing room. Before sealing us, however, he spoke to us for a while and offered some advice, sharing moments of his marriage with his sweetheart, Camilla, with us. As best I can remember, he said:

> Now, everybody thinks that Camilla and I have a perfect marriage. But we still have to work on it. We still have problems and disagreements. We talk about them, and we pray about them, and the Lord helps us work them out. You have to recognize that you're always going to have problems that you have to solve. You're always being tested. You two think that you're in love today, but problems will arise, and you'll have to work at keeping your marriage strong, just like Sister Kimball and I have to work at ours.

Just after offering this advice, he turned to me and said, "Is there anything else you'd like me to say, Jake?" And I said, "Well, no President Kimball. I'm not in the habit of telling Prophets what to say." And he said, "All right," then he sealed us. Then he told me to kiss the bride, which I did, and then he got a little twinkle in his eye.

"Do I get to kiss the bride?" he asked.

"Of course, President Kimball."

"Oh, thank you. You know, the temple is the only place where I get to kiss beautiful young ladies." And he stepped over to Kathleen and kissed her on the cheek. Then he went around the room and shook everybody's hand and introduced himself. Then he came back to us.

"Can I kiss her on the cheek one more time before I leave?" he asked.

"Of course, President Kimball."

He kissed Kathleen one more time then excused himself from us. The spirit that dwelt with us in the sealing room was simply the most beautiful, peaceful spirit I have ever felt. As we left the temple to begin our married lives together, there was absolutely no question, no doubt, that we had done the right thing and that *all* those involved, on this side of the veil and on the other, were pleased.

It shouldn't surprise anybody that our first son is named Matthew Spencer.

As President Kimball told us, we have had to work on our marriage. Peace and harmony can be elusive commodities in this world, but with our commitments to each other and to the children, we have been able to find that peace and harmony far more often than not.

I believe in President McKay's great words: "No other success can compensate for failure in the home." Each Wednesday certain Senators hold a prayer breakfast for all those in the Senate who are interested. Although I am not always able to be there, I try to make it when I can and have been invited to lead it once or twice a year. Although only fifteen to eighteen Senators seem to want to attend, we have some excellent talks and discussions and always come away feeling better about ourselves and each other. It's been an excellent opportunity to put differences aside and come together as sons and daughters of God. When it's my turn to lead the discussion, however, some of the members feign hardship; they know that I'm going to talk about family. They complain that I'm a big, broken record, but I do it anyway. I find scriptures in the Bible to back up my points, and I stress the relative unimportance of all else that we do if we fail in the homes. Thinking back on it, some of my best talks have probably come in these prayer breakfasts on the importance of family. I don't know if I have changed anybody's feelings—most of those attending the breakfasts are already committed to their families—but I don't think we can stress this point enough. We need to leaven our work periodically with the reminder of *why* we're working so hard. As President McKay said, we should be working for our families.

There are times, though, when family needs conflict with our personal needs—or what we think are personal needs. I've been a licensed airplane pilot for practically as long as I can remember. I love flying. I've flown for the Navy, for the Air National Guard, and of course for my own enjoyment. There came a time not too long ago, though, when I had to decide between spending my time flying or spending it with the family. It eventually became

17

one of the hardest decisions I've had to make. I was a Colonel in the Air National Guard, and flying had consumed much of my time on weekends away from the Senate in Salt Lake. I was part of a regular crew on a KC-135 which flew tanker missions, and it was something I looked forward to virtually every week. Finally, Kathleen said to me one day (I think she said it jokingly, but I know there was a lot of truth in it): "You've got me, and you've got the United States Senate, and you've got the Air National Guard. You can keep two out of three."

I retired from the Air National Guard. But I really suffered in making that decision. Of course I would never jeopardize my family for a pastime or anything else, but I really loved flying those big planes and being part of a crew and feeling its camaraderie. When I realized the family was being hurt by it, though, I had to let it go.

I believe that families are forever. This time on earth is fleeting, more fleeting sometimes than we may know, or be prepared for. There comes a time when we all have to let go, when we have to leave this world and embrace the world to come. How grateful I am that I have my family waiting for me there. Without that knowledge, the short span of life here would seem almost meaningless.

I saw my parents enjoy their golden wedding anniversary before my father passed away. I saw their contentment and quiet joy in his last years, the commitment to each other, and in a way, the preparation for a new life to come. My father had developed prostate cancer a few years before, which eventually developed into bone cancer. As he gradually became weaker, I was able to see the compassion and devotion that my mother had for him. She was in ill-health herself, suffering from a weak heart, high blood pressure, and worsening cataracts, but she never let these things stop her from caring for her husband. After taking him in and out of the hospital for a year or so and seeing no improvement, she declared that she was keeping him at home where she could care for him full-time.

Although she was seventy-five years old, she brought a hospital bed into the house for him and tended to him better than most nurses. Dad tried to be stoic through all this, but we could see that he was suffering greatly. The pain had become unbearable, and the decision was finally reached by the doctors to severe his spinal cord so that he couldn't feel the pain anymore. It was agonizing to see him waste away a little each day, a man who had stood strong and tall for so many years now reduced to less than ninety pounds and almost completely paralyzed. I went by their home everyday and helped turn him and spent as much time visiting him as I could.

This was during my campaign for mayor of Salt Lake City, and we spent many hours discussing the race and my work as a City Commissioner and what the future held. I took the children up often, and he was very patient with them, telling them stories and visiting with them one by one. My mother was always nearby, ready to attend him in any way she could.

One day when we were visiting about the mayoral campaign, which had become a very difficult and unhappy one because of his condition, he turned to me and said, "I don't know why you want to do this, but you'll win. I know you'll be elected." He didn't live to see his prophecy fulfilled.

About two weeks later the doctors said that he didn't have much time, maybe a few days, so my sisters and I went to their home that evening to stay with Mother and him. He lapsed into a coma that night, and we spent the next day, which was Saturday, just watching over him and comforting Mother. Because the bedrooms were full, I spent that night and the next on the couch in the living room. Sunday night I had been up watching him until late and had gone to bed quite tired. The next morning, though, I woke up with a start at seven o'clock. I wasn't tired at all, and I noticed that it was a beautiful, clear day outside. Suddenly I knew that I needed to get to the bedroom, so I ran out of the living room to my parent's room. As I entered the doorway I saw that Mother was sound asleep next to him. I went around the bed and I took his hand. His circulation had been fading, and his hands were cooler than would be expected. His face was absolutely serene, as it had been the whole time he had been in the coma. Then without any other movements, he opened his eyes, looked at me and said, "I love you, Son."

Then he closed his eyes and died.

I held his hand for a moment longer, still watching him, then realizing that I had been called in there to let him tell me good-bye. Something had spoken to me, perhaps spirit to spirit, and pulled me out of that exhausted sleep and told me to get into the bedroom. As soon as I was there, my father came out of his coma, for the first time in three days, and told me he loved me. I felt a closeness to him then that I could never describe. We had always been close, but at that moment I felt like I knew him, not only as a father, but as a kindred spirit—a close friend. My mother woke up then, and I told her that Dad was gone.

We all must leave this world, but how wonderful to go with family by our sides, on this side of the veil, and on the other. How wonderful to receive love, and to give it, and know that it will exist forever. How wonderful to know that the gospel of

Jesus Christ is true and that all its promises are there for us if we'll only be faithful. I love my father, and I love my mother, and I love my first wife, Hazel, all who are now gone, and I await the day when I can be with them again. And I look forward to the day when I can have all my family there, Kathleen and all our children, living in celestial glory within the extended family of our God and Father. I look forward to us all living there, reunited with the Family we once left.

With my first wife,
Hazel Rhae Thompson.
(Photo by Saans Photography.
Used by permission.)

With my wife,
Kathleen Brewerton.
(Photo by Busath Photography.
Used by permission.)

. . . In Tolerance and Love

I come from a long line of active Mormons. In fact, my great grandfather Garn, Daniel Garn, was a bodyguard for Joseph Smith and later the first mission president in Germany, in 1852. Each of my eight great grandparents came to Utah before the railroad in 1869, and my ancestors on my mother's side helped settle Sanpete County. Despite that background, however, it seems that every generation has to learn what's right and what's wrong for itself. My grandfather Christensen displayed some of these characteristics.

Although he came of firm-rooted Mormon stock, he picked up the habit of smoking cigars somewhere, and he had a difficult time quitting. Because of this, he rarely came to church. He felt that he would be judged harshly by others, and although he knew that the Church was true, he forfeited having many of its blessings because of this habit. Then he got what one might call an enlightened bishop. He came to my grandfather and said, "Brother Christensen, you ought to be in Church." My grandfather said, "Well, Bishop, I'd like to, but I smoke cigars." The bishop didn't let this deter him. He came right back and said, "I can understand your feelings; we don't want you smoking cigars, and we'd like you to quit, but we'd much rather have you in Church." After that, I can remember my grandfather going to church most every Sunday. All he needed was some positive reenforcement. After my grandfather realized that the bishop wouldn't judge him harshly, in fact, that the bishop *wanted* him in church, he found his way back through the doors again. I also remember him leaving between priesthood and Sunday School for a few minutes to puff on his cigar. He knew he had a bad habit, but once he felt the acceptance and love of the bishop, he made sure he came to church.

I know that the Word of Wisdom is absolutely true—that it's a commandment from God—but I also believe that a lot of people have been forced out of the Church by intolerant friends and family members who embarrass them, or aggravate them, because of their weaknesses. I know that my grandfather would probably not have come back to church if he had not had an understanding bishop. He could have sat out his whole life and not enjoyed many of the blessings of the gospel. As it was, coming back to church gave him new determination to overcome his habit, and with a lot of hard work, and encouragement from the family, he finally quit smoking. Tolerance paid great rewards. As I got older, I was to learn that he was a wonderful human being and that his strengths in other areas were much greater than his weakness in that one. Over the years he set a very important example for me. He had a lot to offer to the Church and to the family. I hate to think that we could have lost that influence if a wise bishop had not intervened.

I've learned that tolerating a person's weakness is not the same as condoning it. I know that the standards of the gospel are inviolable, but I also know that there is no greater virtue than pure love. We really can love a person who disobeys commandments. In fact, we must. Tolerance too is a commandment. It is one of the most difficult commandments that I have ever tried to learn.

I remember some years ago complaining to the bishop that everybody came to church late. I said, "Now, maybe this is none of my business, but if you'll just start the meeting on time, everybody will start getting here on time." He looked at me a moment and said, "Well, Brother Garn, I think you're right. I think I'll try it." Then to get the members motivated, he invited me to speak in sacrament meeting on punctuality. Of course, I had to talk—I was trapped. I gave the talk, and now I'm trapped for life. I can't dare be late—not after that talk. Even if there's a good reason, I can't let the members see me come into the chapel late. If the family is running a little slow that morning, or if there's some small emergency, I have to take another car and get there on time—even if it means breaking the traffic laws to do it. It's a miserable feeling, being trapped for life—all because of intolerance.

Years before that, I learned another humbling lesson about tolerance. I was trying to convince my children to be good and to obey their parents. The example I was using was myself. I knew that I had been a good child, and I couldn't understand how they could be so disobedient. They didn't believe that I had always obeyed my parents, however, so to prove to them that I was the angel I claimed, I took them outside and marched them all up the street and around the corner to my mother's home. I knew that she would back me up.

We went in and I said, "Mother, isn't it true that the reason you never put any restrictions on me was because I never really gave you any problem—you didn't have to force me to go to church, and you didn't have to force me to go to school or do my homework, and when I went out at night with friends I would always tell you who I was going out with, and if we were going to be late, I'd always get to a phone and tell you what happened and how much longer it'd be before I got home, and I got all my priesthood stickers for one hundred percent attendance, and everything else. Now, would you tell my kids that I'm not just using this as an example—that it really is true." Then my mother looked at them and said with a smile, "Your father is telling the truth. He was always an odd child."

My children laughed out loud. Then they asked her if that was true, that I was always an odd child. And she said, "Yes, his father and I used to worry about him. We thought that kids got in trouble once in a while, you know, got home late now and then, or got behind in their schoolwork, but he never did. He never even got sent to his room. It wasn't normal." The kids laughed again, and I knew that my lesson had backfired. Tolerance and patience, I found out, would have paid much greater dividends than preaching to my children.

I only wish I could have learned this lesson long before I did. Even after my children were teenagers, I had trouble accepting them for exactly what they were—my own precious children, faults and all. I learned many hard lessons. Unfortunately, one of these lessons came after the most difficult trial of my life.

I share this only after much consideration—and with permission from my son. As great as my trial was, his was greater.

When my oldest son, Jake, was fifteen, I found out that he was smoking marijuana. I'll never forget that day; I asked Jake to get into the car and go for a ride with me. We drove up to a nearby park and got out and sat on the grass. I said, "Jake, I've heard you've been experimenting with pot." He started to cry, then he said, "Yeah, Dad, I have. I'm really sorry." We ended up having a nice talk about how harmful drugs could be to us and what would happen if we ever got addicted to something like marijuana—even if it was just a psychological addiction. We also talked about the Church and what the Lord expected of us as his children.

I had a reputation with some of my kids of being too tough on them, and I remembered thinking that I had finally overcome that. When we got home, my wife, Hazel, said, "Well, did you get mad at him?" And I said no. Jake overheard this and came in and said, "No, Mom, as a matter of fact, Dad was really nice," and he turned to me and said, "Thanks, Dad." At that point I thought I had solved two problems: my temper and his experimentation with marijuana. Within a short time, however, it was clear that neither had really been overcome.

Two or three years later, it was evident that his problem with drugs had progressed to really affect and dominate his life. He was growing increasingly argumentative, and his work at school was suffering. It seemed that each day he was becoming a greater challenge for the family. But, despite these changes, I thought that his problem was controllable. I really thought that with time, his feelings would change and he would return to the happy, successful young man we had always known. Then the saddest day of his life, and mine, came.

I was in Salt Lake City, and the family was preparing to drive back to Washington to begin school at the end of the summer. The night before the family left, he and his mother had an argument that just kind of exploded. This really wasn't like her—she'd always been so kind and gentle—but she was just so frustrated with his behavior and his use of drugs that, in a moment of anger, she said: "I'm sorry I ever gave birth to you."

That was the last thing he ever heard her say. The next day I received the word from the Nebraska Highway Patrol that my wife had been killed. While sobbing almost uncontrollably, I embraced him and told him that his mother was dead. He didn't cry; he didn't say anything. In that moment, I think something inside him snapped. The next few years would be the most trying of our lives, and with the grief that I was experiencing myself, it was almost more than I could bear.

He completely left the Church and renounced any belief in God. Then he left the house and found a dingy apartment in downtown Salt Lake. Now, not only could I not help him daily, I couldn't even talk to him. Friends who had seen him told me that he was letting his hair grow longer and that he looked stoned most of the time. I was worried that he might be killed or hurt badly because of his drug habit and the people he hung around. They said that he had become very paranoid, and that he wouldn't look at people, and that he would disappear for periods of time. Even my mother, who had always had a close relationship with him, tried to talk with him but wasn't able to get anywhere. I tried to communicate with him but wasn't successful, and I increasingly became more concerned.

I spent much time in prayer then, and I know that the Lord helped me feel some peace, but I still didn't know what to do. I felt that I was losing more than my son, I felt like a part of myself was being wrenched away. I would sit in Senate hearings in those days, appearing to be listening, but inside I was agonizing over how to save my oldest son. Then I decided to take drastic measures. I called the LDS Hospital and had him involuntarily committed for psychiatric evaluation. I was able to get a hold of Jake first, and I told him what I had done, that I would take him, by force if necessary, to the hospital. He seemed to understand my feelings, and, fortunately, went with me voluntarily.

After he had been there a short while, the diagnosis came back: he had congenital brain damage. I couldn't believe it. I cried for a couple of days after that, wishing that I had been able to help him sooner, wondering what I could have done differently. He had been a good kid, a good student, active in the Church, until his drug use. And I figured that that's what damaged his brain, since he had been completely normal until he started taking them. So I went to Jake and said, "You might as well know what the diagnosis is. They said that your behavior indicates congenital brain damage." He just said, "Oh, no Dad. I had one of my friends sneak some pot into me; I've been high the whole time I've been in here."

Believe it or not, I was actually relieved.

A short time later Jake came back home, in Salt Lake, and we began talking more often. This wasn't necessarily good, though, because we argued so much. When I was in Washington, we argued on the phone. When I was in Salt Lake, we argued in person. We argued for hours, and some of the arguments became quite bitter. I found myself hoping that something would happen to him, and I kept thinking, "I just can't cope with this anymore; I just can't cope with this anymore." I feel guilty now, looking back on it, because I became so desperate. A normal, rational conversation between the two of us was nearly impossible. He was convinced that I was wrong, and I knew that he was wrong. And this went on month after month.

During this difficult time, I married Kathleen, and she saw just how negative the situation had become. She was bothered by the arguments but tried to show love for us both. I could see what kind of position I was putting her in, but I didn't know how to avoid it. She had assumed great responsibility in helping me raise my four children, and she was remarkable. My problems with Jake were so great that I couldn't see how to handle the other problems around it. Without Kathleen's amazing support, I could never have survived this period in my life.

One evening my mother called me over to her house and said she wanted to talk to me. She said that she had been watching Jake and me, and she had some advice for me.

"First of all," she said, "he is worth saving. Right now you're going about everything all wrong. You're arguing with him too much. You're trying to talk to him logically, but that isn't going to help. And then when he disagrees, you say that he's wrong. Can't you see, Jake, he doesn't think you love him anymore." I sat still, thinking about what she had said. "Now, I'm no psychiatrist—I didn't even go to college," she continued, "but I think you need to separate your love for your son and your sadness for his mistakes. I think you need to let him know that you love him but disapprove of his actions."

I had spent thousands of dollars on doctors, but this sounded like the best advice I'd heard so far, so I went home determined to try it. At first, it wasn't too hard; I found that if I avoided arguing with him, my emotions didn't get involved and I was able to stay on an even keel. If he got mad at me for my responses to his questions, I'd just say, "Hey, son, don't ask my advice if you don't want it." But I would add, "if you do ask for my advice, I'm going to give you the best answer I've got. What you do with it is your business." He couldn't argue with that. There were times, of course, when things got more complicated, but I never raised my voice at him again. There was the time when he traded his car, which was virtually brand new, for one that was beat up and worth about half the value. It took great control not to blow up at him over that one; eventually I went down to the man who had made the trade and got mad at him, but I was able to keep my temper with Jake.

We were having a lot of phone calls then, with me in Washington most of the time and he in Salt Lake, but the tenor of them changed: he would argue and throw insults, and I would listen and try to control my emotions. This was never easy, but I felt that I had to do it to really give our relationship the best chance I could. It was hard to say, "I love you, Jake, but I don't approve of the things you're doing," or, "I love you, Jake, but I don't appreciate the way you're speaking right now." The natural man, I guess, wanted to rise up and do battle, but I had to keep fighting it down. Then one night I got a call from my daughter, Sue, who was going to the University of Utah. She said, "I don't know what you're doing, Dad, but keep doing it, because Jake does everything you say. I hear his side of the conversation, and I know how hard it must be to take the verbal abuse, but keep doing it, because when he hangs up he tries to do exactly what

31

you say. He just doesn't want you to have the satisfaction of knowing that he's following your advice."

I called my mother and said, "You're right. He's changing." And she said, "That's right, son, when you stopped being part of the problem, he began changing."

These calls from him continued, and I just hoped that what my daughter and mother had seen in him was true, because at the time I couldn't tell much change at all. Then I got a call from him one night. He was crying, and he said, "Dad, I need help."

I said, "Oh, son, I've been waiting a long time to hear that." And he asked me what I wanted him to do. I didn't hesitate; I said, "Son, get in your car and drive back to Washington." "But I'm registered for school at the 'U'," he said, and I said, "I don't care about that. Forget school for now. Come back." He was twenty years old and was finally coming home again.

Things were quite tense at first. Although he recognized that he needed help, he wasn't willing to drop all the walls he had erected. One night at the dinner table, I had just finished saying the blessing on the food when he said, "I don't have to listen to that b---s---. I don't believe in that. There is no God." I was taken back, but Kathleen looked him square in the eye and said: "Jake, I want to tell you something. You don't have to believe what your father and I believe. You don't even have to listen to us pray. You can sit there and plug your ears and wait until the blessing is over, but as long as you're sitting at your father's table, and eating his food, you'll sit there and keep your mouth shut."

It was as if he had been hit between the eyes with a two-by-four. He just said, "Uh, all right."

A while later his grandmother, Hazel's mother, Rhae Thompson, came back to visit us, and Jake was going through his story again, talking on about how God was a myth and the Church was terrible and Joseph Smith was a nut, and so on. And his grandmother was the perfect lady; she just sat there and listened to it all. When he was through, he said, "Well, what do you think of that, Grandma?" And she said, "I think that's a bunch of b---s---, Jake." It was like another two-by-four. That was the last thing in the world he was expecting from her, and it may have made him think a little.

One of consequences of Jake's lifestyle had been a deterioration of his self-confidence. He was afraid of trying anything new, and so work was difficult for him. I got him a job with Senator Paul Laxalt, from Nevada, helping with correspondence in his office. Jake came back from work that first night and said that the job was too tough. He said, "They want me to read letters and answer them, and I don't know how to write letters. I want you to call Senator Laxalt and tell him I'm going to quit." I told him that he had to do his own quitting. So he went in the next day to tell the senator, and when I got home that evening I asked how it had gone. He said, "Senator Laxalt won't let me quit. He said that you got me the job and I have to keep it until he cans me." So Jake kept going into work, supposedly to write the correspondence for the senator. I found out later, though, that the letters he wrote initially weren't going anywhere. Senator Laxalt was just keeping him on to help get his confidence back. I really appreciate him for that. Eventually, Jake got so that he really could help in the office, and as he became more proficient in the office, his self-esteem gradually improved.

After a year, he went back to Utah and reentered college. He was still having problems with drugs but it wasn't nearly as serious as it had been. In fact, he called me every time he slipped up. He'd say, "I smoked a little pot today, Dad. I'm sorry." The relationship between us was entirely different, even though there were those problems. Then, a year later, he called with an unusual request. He wanted to know when I would be back in Utah. I said it would be a couple of weeks, then asked him why. "Well, I'd like to go to church," he said, "and I don't want to go alone." After a moment of silence he said, "I want to go with you—like we used to." I told him that I'd be happy to go to church with him, and then he added, "But I don't want to be asked to do anything." I told him that I didn't think that would be any problem. Just to be sure, though, I called the bishop and got everything squared away with him, making sure that people wouldn't make a big deal of Jake being there, or ask him to offer the prayer. I asked the bishop just to let things happen natural-ly—to come with time. So I went to church with him a couple weeks later and everybody treated him like he had been there all along, nothing unusual, just a lot of nice handshakes and welcomes. On the way home he said, "This doesn't mean I'm going to go all the time." I just had to chuckle inside. I said, "Hey, I know, you're a big boy now, twenty-two years old, you can make up your own mind. Of course, I'd like you to go to church, but that's your business." I was using Mother's technique again.

I called one of his friends who was a returned missionary and asked him to be a spy for me. Since I was spending most of my time in Washington, I needed someone else to check on Jake's progress. The next Sunday, the friend called and said, "Well, he came to church today by himself." The next week the same thing happened. Then the next. And pretty soon, he was totally active. He didn't miss a single Sunday after that. About five months later I got a call from another of his friends, John Homer, who said, "Brother Garn, you've got to help me. Jake is driving me crazy. We're home teaching companions, and if we don't get our home teaching done by the tenth of each month, he's all over me. He doesn't let up. You've got to help him mellow out, Brother Garn." I was delighted. I told him that I was sorry about the inconvenience but that he had to put up with it for a while, for Jake's sake.

A few weeks later Jake came home for Christmas, and he took me off alone in the house and asked me to sit down. I was suspicious and asked him why I had to sit down. "Because I'm going to shock you," he said. So I sat down and he said, "Dad, I want to go on a mission." I thought about this for a moment then said, "Son, are you sure you want to go on a mission, or do you just want to please Dad." He said that he really wanted to go on a mission, that he wanted to serve the Lord. I was still suspicious. I called Jon Huntsman, who was serving as a mission president in the Washington DC area, and asked him if Jake couldn't spend some time going on splits with the missionaries. I was pretty sure that this would make Jake show his hand. There's nothing like knocking on a few hundred doors to help a man be honest with himself. Jon was delighted to have Jake serve with his missionaries. So Jake spent two weeks tracting with the missionaries, going to their meetings, getting rejections, bearing testimony, and at the end of that time he said, "Dad, I still want to serve a mission." Well, I still wasn't convinced, so I told him to go back to Utah and think about it some more. Going on a two-year mission would be the hardest thing he ever did, and with his past, I told him, I wasn't even sure that he would be allowed to go. So Jake went back to Utah, and in a few weeks I got a call from Elder Neal A. Maxwell. We had known each other for some time, but still it wasn't every day that I got a call from him. He said, Jake, are you going to let your son go on a mission?" And I said, "I don't know Elder Maxwell, he's done a lot of things wrong, and I don't want him to serve a mission as a penance. I'm not sure he's prepared to go for the right reasons." Then he told me that he had just interviewed Jake and that he was convinced of Jake's sincerity and worthiness to serve. He said, "Let him go, Jake. Let him go. I've never heard a boy come in and be so honest and frank. He told me things I didn't expect to hear, but he just opened up and gave the most total confession I've ever heard. He probably told me things that you don't even know about. Please, Jake, let him go. He's ready."

Of course, when a General Authority encourages you to do something, you don't just consider it—you do it. So I gave Jake my blessing and told him that we would support him in everything he did, provided it was within the rules. He sent in his papers and was called to serve in the England Coventry Mission. At his farewell he gave one of the most moving talks I've ever heard. He had come a long way from the disbelieving, disobedient teenager of just a few years ago. In a voice that left few dry eyes in the congregation, He said: "Brothers and sisters, most of you know the hell that my father has gone through in losing my mother. But what many of you don't know is the hell that I've put him through for the last few years with my drug problems. What I want you all to know is that even though I didn't deserve it, my father kept loving me. Despite his own suffering, and despite my rebellion, he kept loving me."

As he said this, I just cried. And I thought of my mother who had just recently passed away. I wanted to embrace her, to say, "Oh, Mother, you dear, sweet soul, you always knew, didn't you? You told me to love him, to stop fighting him, to separate his deeds from the fact that he was my son. You told me, Mother, that he was worth saving; and *now* look at him! It was love that saved him, Mother, love and tolerance. And you knew all along. You knew from the beginning." It was one of the most emotional moments in my life.

He went to England and became one of the most dedicated elders that they had ever had. In fact, he may have become too dedicated. I got a note from his mission president once that I needed to write my son about a problem he was having. I sat there and thought, oh no, what has he done? I called the president and said, "What is it, President. What is he doing?" The president said, "Well, basically, he's driving the other elders crazy. He's so meticulous in following the rules that they can't stand to be around him sometimes. I was looking at one of his reports the other day and I noticed that he had deducted twenty-five minutes from his tracting time. So I called him in and asked him what this was all about. He said, 'Well, we were passing out Books of Mormon, and I didn't plan carefully enough and we ran out. So my companion and I had to run back and get more, which took twenty-five minutes, so I deducted that from our tracting time.' Brother Garn, I know he wants to serve the Lord, but can you drop him a letter and tell him to loosen up a little bit?" So I sent him a letter and said that although I had encouraged him to obey the rules, there were times when he needed to loosen up, to be sensitive to others, and that maybe he didn't need to be so meticulous in his reports.

Again, it was a matter of tolerance, only this time it was Jake who needed to learn it. We all have convictions, and there are times when our zeal in honoring those convictions causes us to lose perspective, to lose sight of our ultimate goal. That's what had happened to me in those long years of contention with my son. I had absolutely the courage of my convictions—I knew he was wrong and I was right—but I had lost sight of my true goal, to bring my family back to our Father in heaven. It was love that brought him back, and I had lost that love and replaced it with severity and demands. I had tried to compel him to follow the Father's plan.

Toward the end of his mission, he wrote me a letter and said that he had broken a rule. Again, I sat there and thought, "Oh no, he's only got two months left; what's he done now?" The letter went on and recounted how he had been the mission financial secretary for a long time and how he had wanted so badly to get out of the mission home and be a teaching companion again. And finally he had gotten his wish and was just so excited that he couldn't wait for P-day to write this letter and let me know. This was his violation of the rules. Again, I just had to smile. What a wonderful son I had. He may not have loosened up much, but his heart was in the right place.

I flew over to England to pick him up at the end of his mission. We attended a meeting in Coventry for all the missionaries who had completed their service, and at this meeting a

woman came up and said that my son had saved her life. I was
a little surprised and asked her if I had heard her right, and she
repeated that, yes, Elder Garn had saved her life. We weren't able
to visit about it then, so on the plane home I asked my son about
it. He tried to shrug it off and said that it wasn't like that, that he
hadn't saved her life at all. I asked him to share the whole
incident with me. The story he related has strengthened my
testimony and made me doubly grateful for the small part I
played in preparing him to serve the Lord. I'll share it here as he
shared it with me.

We were in Lincoln, and it was about eight o'clock at
night, and was cold and wet. My new junior companion
had been out about three weeks, and he said, "Elder
Garn, let's go back to our flat; we're just getting soaked.
Let's just call it a day." We were standing at the entrance
of a roundabout, with five streets leading off it, and I just
felt strongly that we needed to knock on a few more
doors. I said, "No, Elder, we're not going back yet. I feel
impressed that we need to go down one more street and
knock on a few more doors, and then we'll go home for
the night." I didn't know which street we were to go
down, so I just bowed my head and asked the Lord for
his guidance, and when I opened my eyes I had a very
distinct impression to go down a particular street, one of
those leading off the roundabout.

We got about halfway down the street when we found a
lady unloading bags of groceries from her car. We asked
her if we could help her take the groceries into the house,

and she said yes. After helping her, we told her that we were missionaries and asked if we could share our message with her. She listened to it, and as a result, she took all the lessons and gained a testimony and was baptized. Eventually her entire family joined the Church. But what we didn't know was her side of the story. After her baptism, she told us.

She said that she had been very depressed because of problems with her husband and family. She felt that life just wasn't worth going on. So she had gone to the store to get groceries for her family and then she was going to commit suicide. On the way home, though, she said a silent prayer, asking the Lord to send somebody to help her. A few minutes later, we showed up. I know that it wasn't a coincidence that I felt impressed to go down that particular street. The Lord found a way to speak to me, and through me to her.

I didn't think my love and respect for my son could grow anymore than it had during the time he served his mission, but when he told me this story on the way home, my love seemed limitless. He had become an instrument in the hands of the Lord, not just to preach the gospel, but to follow the Spirit and bless the lives of others, wherever they might have been. I saw the love in that woman's eyes, the eternal gratitude she had for him. He had been willing to go the extra mile to find that one soul who was ready for the gift of life that he had to offer. I don't think a father could have a finer son. Today Jake has a wonderful wife who served a mission in Switzerland and three beautiful children. Besides holding a B.A. in accounting and an M.B.A. from the University of Utah, he is a Certified Public Accountant and is managing a very successful career. Not only has he grown into a fine son, but he has become a great husband and father.

My mother told me to love him. She said to stop being part of the problem, and the problem would take care of itself. I had to put the "courage of my convictions" on hold for a while, long enough for my son to discover his own convictions—and his own courage. I had to let him suffer on his own, to bear his own cross, and then, like a greater Father, I had to be available to bring him home when the time came. This boy had to become a man in his own way, and now that he is, I find that I can take little credit for it. All I did was love him.

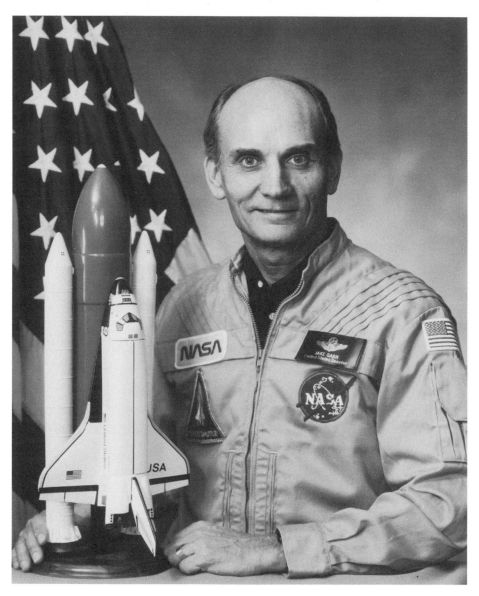

This portrait was taken in 1985, at the time of my flight aboard Discovery.
(Photo courtesy NASA. Used by permission of Jake Garn.)

. . . In the Family of Man

My father had only one requirement for me in life—I absolutely had to become a pilot. He didn't care what else I did in life, but I *had* to become a pilot. A pilot in World War I, he had purchased his first airplane before I was born and knew people like Amelia Earhart and Jimmy Doolittle. He went on to became a pioneer of aviation himself, serving as Regional Airport Supervisor for the Bureau of Air Commerce in the eleven Western states (the predecessor of the FAA) and then being named the first Utah Director of Aeronautics. Flying seemed to be in his blood, and, fortunately for me, it seemed to be in my blood too. I took to it as fast as he did.

My mother used to wonder aloud what sin she had committed to have both a husband and son who flew airplanes. She *hated* flying; she would only go on a commercial airliner if she were coaxed, and even then it was white knuckles all the way. We probably took a few years off her life every time both of us went up together.

By the time I was a little boy, I knew I had to fly, and when the time came for me to enter the service I knew that there were only two options: flying for the Navy or flying for the Air Force.

Somewhere along the line I heard that flying for the Navy was more exciting and glamorous, so I decided to become a Naval aviator. Looking back at it, I don't know if it made that much difference since I switched later in life and began flying for the Utah Air National Guard, a division of the Air Force. Both have been real blessings in my life. In fact, without them, I never would've had one of the greatest experiences in my life—an experience that magnified my testimony of God in more ways than I can share.

When STS-1 flew—that was Columbia, the first space shuttle—I told Jim Beggs, the administrator of NASA, that I wanted to fly on the Shuttle. He said, "Hey, so do I, so does everybody." And I said, "No, not everybody, not like I do." He looked at me with a little smile and said, "You're serious, aren't you?" And I said, "Yes, I'm serious, and I'm qualified, too." I reminded him that I had as much pilot flight time as most of the astronauts, that I was an Air Force Colonel, that I had flown most of the big airplanes, including the B-1, that I had flown from aircraft carriers as a Naval aviator. "And besides," I added, "this would help me in my responsibilities as Chairman of the Senate committee overseeing NASA." He just chuckled, but I told him that I was going to keep bugging him until he let me go.

I already knew most of the astronauts because I was at NASA frequently in my capacity on the Senate subcommittee. I had worked with General Tom Stafford and Russian General Leonav in the Apollo-Soyuz joint mission in 1975 and had even flown dockings in the simulator. Once, when John Young was in space, I was in Australia where NASA had a tracking station, and I took the opportunity to visit with him over the radio. I said, "Hi, John, this is Senator Garn, and I still expect to be up there someday with you." When I got back to Washington Jim Beggs came up to me said, I understand you're talking with the astronauts in space now, trying to convince them that you're going up with them." I said, "I just don't want you to ever forget, Jim."

And he didn't. Despite the razzing I took from everybody who knew about this dream of mine, the day finally came when Jim came to me in my Senate office in the fall of 1984.

I was working in my office when Jim came in and sat down. I looked up at him and said what I'd said a hundred times, "When are you going to let me fly, Jim?" He said, "I don't know, how about January?" I went right on talking until I realized what he had said. "What did you say?" He said, "I've decided to let you go, but I've got a problem."

At this point I decided that no problem was going to get in my way, and I asked him what it was.

"I don't want every member of Congress asking to go on the Space Shuttle," he said.

I told him that I had a solution. "Don't invite people," I said, "invite positions. Issue invitations to the chairmen of the House and Senate Authorizing Committees and the House and Senate Appropriations Subcommittees—those who have oversight responsibility for NASA. That's only four invitations."

"How many do you think will go?" he asked.

"None—except me."

And they didn't, until Congressman Bill Nelson assumed one of the positions in the House the next year.

But, of course, people thought they saw politics involved. The day after it was announced that I was going, Jane Pauley interviewed me on the *Today* show. "Isn't it true," she said, "that the only reason you're going into space is because you're Chairman of NASA's Appropriation Subcommittee?" And I said, "Of course," and that blew all the steam out of her interview. I told her that I didn't make any apology for going, that I was an experienced military and civilian aviator with over 10,000 hours of pilot time and that, indeed, I was chairman of the committee that appropriated nearly eight billion dollars for the NASA budget—that I had an obligation to be closely involved with their projects. She was very kind to me after that. It's interesting to note that since my flight nobody has tried to pull the wool over my eyes concerning NASA's needs. When anybody testified about space after my shuttle trip, they spoke more specifically and accurately. When Bill Proxmier became chairman of the committee it was interesting how he would turn to me during these hearings and say, "How about that, Jake?" and everybody listened. I became a resource for the legislative body governing NASA's—and therefore the nation's—space expenditures.

We were supposed to fly in February 1985, but we had a series of delays that set us back until April. Far from being a disappointment, this was a blessing because I got to be an astronaut longer. I found myself waking up at night feeling like it was Christmas Eve, that Santa Claus was on his way. I felt like pinching myself sometimes; I just couldn't believe that I was walking around with a blue NASA flight suit on, with my fellow astronauts. We were quarantined a couple of times—where they seclude us for a week so we don't take any viruses or illnesses into space—but more delays came up and we went back to normal training.

I was originally scheduled to fly on Challenger, the Shuttle that blew up. Our last cancellation, however—due to malfunctions in the satellite we were to take up—caused us to be shifted to the Space Shuttle Discovery. We never did take that TDRS satellite up; it went up later with its original ship, Challenger, and was destroyed. Because of all the training, I became very close with the Challenger crew. Mike Smith, the pilot of Challenger, was my trainer, and Dick Scoby, the Commander, had become a personal friend. I don't think I'll ever be able to express the grief and sadness I felt when I saw that craft explode that morning. It was as if a part of me had died along with my friends.

Exactly four years to the day from when the first Shuttle had gone up—it was now April 12, 1985—we were on the launch pad, strapped to our seats in 90 degree positions. We had made it through quarantine and were now completely alone on the pad. Because of the enormous volatility of the fuel that we were sitting on, no one else, no engineers, no fire-fighting crews, *nobody*, was within three and a half miles of us. I remember feeling a strong sense of isolation; right when we might have needed everybody, they were gone.

Then we sat there, and we sat there, and we sat there.

The launch window was three and a half hours long, and we were convinced that we weren't going anywhere. We were in a hold at nine minutes for over three hours. Then, just when we were ready to loose our straps, the okay came over the radio for the countdown to continue. Dave Griggs, up in the flight deck, was already out of his seat and started scrambling to get back in. Because of the complexity in the straps and buckles, we weren't sure he was going to make it. Bo Bobko, our commander, sitting near him, was saying over the intercom, "Are you going to be strapped in, Dave?" And he was saying, "Yes, yes, yes, I'll make it!" And the countdown continued.

My pulse rate climbed dramatically. I was hooked up to blood-pressure and pulse-monitoring devices, which I was watching with amazement. Even though my resting pulse rate is normally forty-eight, it was escalating then to over a hundred. As the countdown went to 10-9-8-7, my pulse rate jumped to 126, and I had just lain there for three hours.

When the main engines ignited, my pulse rate probably flew off the chart. The main engines kicked in at 6.8 seconds prior to launch, and as they spooled up, it felt like the whole earth was shaking. Those engines have a million pounds of thrust, and the orbiter was straining to leave the launch pad. To put this in perspective, a 747 jumbo jet has about forty thousand pounds of thrust in its engines, and it's free to move. We were tied down, and the vibrations and noise were enormous. At "zero," the solid rocket motors ignited, and they produced over three million pounds of thrust each, which produced over seven million pounds of total thrust. I remembered at this point that we would be going someplace for at least two minutes, and I hoped it was in the right direction.

All the tethers came off the orbiter, and I was pressed back into my seat. We only sustained three gs, which is not a lot, but it lasted for a long time. In a jet fighter, you can pull up to nine gs, but it's for only fifteen or twenty seconds. Our three gs lasted for over eight minutes, and the weight seemed to become progressively heavier. Commercial airliners initially climb at about five to seven thousand feet per minute; we were climbing at eighty thousand feet per minute, and accelerating. After three minutes, we had already traveled fifty miles and were committed to go at least to Senegal, in Africa, our first alternate landing site. After six minutes, we were too fast and too high to land at Senegal, and after eight and a half minutes, we were in orbit.

When the main engines complete their burn and the external tanks are discarded to return to earth, the transition to weightlessness is dramatic. After eight and a half minutes of three gs, then sudden weightlessness, you feel like you've gone over the biggest hill on the biggest roller coaster in the universe. Your stomach is anywhere but where it should be, and you're just wondering what it will feel like when you can remove your restraints and float freely. We were over the Indian Ocean by then and were traveling at seventeen thousand, five hundred miles per hour. The orbiter was absolutely quiet. This was the beginning of one of the most sacred and humbling experiences of my life.

Micro gravity kept pulling the orbiter back toward the earth, but the centrifugal force of our speed kept us in orbit. As we rounded the earth every hour and a half, I was struck by the ease of locomotion in the weightless environment. I could do things that the best gymnasts couldn't dream of doing—loops, barrel rolls, multiple flips—but we had to be careful. The first time I put my foot against the bulkhead and gave what I thought was a gentle touch, I became a torpedo and crashed against the opposite wall. I found that I could move myself backwards by just blowing air, and that a fingertip push could propel me faster than I wanted to go. I had the muscles of a hundred and seventy-five pound man, but now I had no weight. During rest periods we had to be velcroed into canvas bags to keep us from floating around the craft. The body naturally goes into a fetal position in a weightless environment, with one's arms slightly above the head and the legs slightly bent. Since there is no down or up, it didn't matter which way our sleeping bags were facing. We just slept as best we could.

The most magnificent sight in space is earth. The first time I got a chance to look out the windows I was awestruck. My breath left me, and I felt that my heart and lungs were going to stop. I couldn't believe how beautiful it was. And of course, added to that was the disbelief of actually being in the vacuum of space. I think that every astronaut goes through the same emotions. We had all seen the films that other astronauts had brought back, films from Gemini and Apollo and other Shuttle flights, but none of us were prepared for the beauty of the earth. In a way, it reminded me of my first experience of looking at the Grand Canyon. Although I had seen pictures of it before, I never understood how large it was, or how magnificently beautiful, until I stood by the rail and looked down into it. Now I was looking down on something that dwarfed everything in my experience. It radiated with light, like it was alive, and the colors were brilliant.

At mach 25, Discovery orbits the earth every hour and a half, giving us sixteen sunrises and sunsets each day—forty-five minutes of daylight followed by forty-five minutes of darkness. The beauty of this spectacle, of the earth itself, is beyond words to describe. Every astronaut comes back to earth with the frustration of not being able to convey the absolute power of the planet's beauty.

Try to imagine seeing the entire Mediterranean Sea at one time, being able to see Spain, Portugal, the Strait of Gibraltar, France, North Africa, Egypt and Israel, the Nile, the Red Sea, the Sinai Peninsula, Saudi Arabia, the Jordan River connecting the Sea of Galilee with the Dead Sea, Lebanon, Turkey, Russia, the Black Sea, the rest of Europe, and beyond that the edge of the earth surrounded by a magnificent rainbow created by the setting sun refracting through the earth's atmosphere. Imagine floating in silence at over seventeen thousand miles per hour and seeing John Glenn's Fireflies sparkling all around the spacecraft. When John flew, NASA didn't know what these dancing specks of light were, but now we know that they are simply frozen ice crystals issuing from excess water in the fuel cells. Imagine this entire picture, a brilliant, white spacecraft surrounded by thousands of dazzling ice crystals, looking down on half the countries of the Northern Hemisphere. The picture becomes magical, unreal, and there isn't an astronaut alive who knows how to describe the awe it produces.

As I looked at this, I *knew* that the earth is alive, and that everything on it is kindred; everything was related. The earth looks absolutely peaceful. No national boundaries are visible, no lines across the continents, no large stars where national capitals should be. From three hundred miles above, Earth looks perfect.

As we gradually orbited the entire planet, I knew that this was a work of sacred creation. And then I felt that I knew, in a small way, the sadness that God must feel for many of his children. We are all creations of the same God, dwelling on the same planet, brothers and sisters with each other, with the earth, and all living things. We are all children of God—we are all family—and from my view I saw just how close that family ought to be. It makes no difference what the color of our skin is or what language we speak; we should try to come together.

My own feelings of anger and sadness surfaced. The Iran-Iraq War was raging then, and as I looked down on that area of the earth, I thought of the Ayatollah and Saddam Hussein, and the tens of thousands of souls being slaughtered. I thought of the hate that infected them like a virus and the absolute mindless, maddening destruction going on because of them. I thought of tyrants like Kaddafi and Idi Amin and wondered why they existed. I wondered how such people could do such barbarous, terrible things to others. And then I had the feeling, and still do, of how incredibly sad and displeased God must be with us. I knew that he had given us this earth to live on, and to keep, and that we were misusing it, each other, and ourselves. We had been given opportunities to dress the earth, as Adam had, but many of us were polluting it. We had been given opportunities to love those around us, as the Savior had, but many of us were squandering our lives in hate and petty grievances. We had been given opportunities to prove ourselves worthy of more light, more trust, but many of us were atrophying in self-absorption and personal weakness. From my vantage point, I saw the whole earth and knew that it was good, and that man was basically good, but that the behavior of God's children is not.

I still have that overwhelming feeling of displeasure, and I find myself wondering why we manage the earth and its resources so badly. How can we live so remarkably short of our abilities? How can we exist in such a sinful state and not exercise the powers in us of forgiveness, love, and self-progression? I looked down at the earth and realized that the majority of our brothers and sisters live in abject poverty—not the kind we define in Congressional halls as so much income per month—but those who literally are starving to death. I looked down at the earth and realized that diseases still ravage the people, diseases that perhaps could be checked if we spent more of our attention on combatting them instead of each other. I looked down at the earth and asked why.

And the answer suddenly was so obvious. It's because we don't obey God's commandments. He created the earth and gave it to us that we might have joy, and he gave us guidelines on how best to attain that joy, but we, for the most part, have neglected that. We have looked for better paths, more satisfying paths, paths that ultimately lead to the suffering and sometimes deaths of ourselves and others. The answer struck me, and it was simple. So simple that I wanted to cry for its absence in our lives.

I became convinced that most people don't see the big picture. I look today at the Arab-Israeli peace talks, and I just think—oh, you little children. You're worried about where, and what time, and who walks in the room first, and what the shape of the table is, but you don't really talk. Maybe you can't agree on the big issues, but you can agree to at least talk about them. You can agree to try, and to recognize that you are all children of God. I firmly believe that if leaders of the governments of this planet could view the earth from space as I have that their attitudes would be very different and the earth would be much more peaceful.

For the first six months that I was back, I was very impatient. I became frustrated at the insignificant things that occupied everybody's minds. I had to relearn patience and to accept people as they are. Now sometimes, when trivial matters keep tripping people up, I want to show them the big picture. I want to show them the potential we have, and the obligations that rest upon us, and the joy and peace we can have if we'll just obey the simple guidelines taught to us by the Creator of this earth.

Struggling with this has probably made me a better person, but I know that I, too, have a long way to go before I reach that incredible peace that I saw resting on the earth. Sometimes in striving for it, I lose the power of it. When I need to dot the i's and cross the t's, I sometimes want to jump to the next important matter, leaving small but important things undone. Peace, the kind I felt in space, comes from doing *all* things in their proper time and proper place. Even God has a proper time and proper place in settling the disputes and ridding the tyrannies of the earth. I find some solace in this, that God will eventually heal the wounds of six thousand years, but I still struggle with our, and my, slow progress in doing our share of God's work on Earth.

People have asked me if I found God in space. The answer is no—I knew him before I went. But there isn't any part of my testimony that wasn't enhanced because of my experience there. My feelings now of progressing eternally, of us being able to become kings and queens and priests and priestesses, have taken on greater meaning. As I looked at the earth, I began to more fully understand the meaning of the priesthood and the partnership with God that we have. I began to really understand that his spirit is within all of us, and in the earth, and that we have a literal responsibility in how we respond to it. I learned that our ultimate responsibility is in how we treat others, that our own joy will come from causing joy and love to grow in others. And as

I looked out at the billions of other stars in space, I realized that God has many children, and that he loves them all, and that they all may be like him. I realized, finally, that there is really no other choice, that if we want peace and joy, we must obey the guidelines he has set. At three hundred miles above the earth, and at seventeen thousand, five hundred miles per hour, I came to know the perfect stillness of a revelation—a revelation of the pain God feels, and of the joy we may yet find in him and in his gospel if we are worthy.

As a young Navy pilot in Japan, 1958.
(Photo courtesy Jake Garn.)

. . . In Freedom and Democracy

I was a typical, sheltered young boy who thought the whole world existed in my back yard. Salt Lake had everything I needed. My family was there, my friends, everything I had ever known. The only traveling we did was to Richfield or to Sanpete County to visit our extended family. Then when I was nineteen my world changed. On a beautiful summer morning some friends and I drove to Bear Lake to go boating and fishing. Before the day was over, we had done something that I felt was quite remarkable. I came in the house that night and found my mother.

"Mother," I said, "You'll never guess what I did today!"

"Hi, Jake, how was the fishing?"

"The fishing was fine, but that isn't it." I'm sure I raised an inch taller as I said, "I went outside the state today. I have now been outside the state of Utah."

"Oh? Where did you go?"

Proud of my adventure, I said, "The guys and I drove across the border into Idaho, and we saw Montpelier!"

That was my first foray into the world beyond my native state, and little did I suspect that it would be followed so soon by adventures around the world. Within a year I had sailed to Europe, Japan, and most of Southeast Asia. By the time I was twenty I knew enough about the world to make me very grateful for my country back home.

I saw a very different existence in those foreign countries, places where the average life expectancy was forty, places where half the children died before the age of one. I saw people catching rain water off their roofs for drinking water. They lived in small shacks—the luckier ones did—that were built on stilts looking over vast swamps. Sanitation was virtually nonexistent, and a varied, healthy diet was impossible. I saw people living as their ancestors had a thousand years before, without technology, without medicine, without entertainment, and ultimately, without security. Their existence not only depended on the luck of their scavengings and small harvests, but on the whims of local and national leaders. Freedom as I had known it in the United States was unheard of in some of those areas. Before serving in the Navy, I had not thought of this much. Although I had known about World War II and the rise of Communism, I was utterly naive concerning the oppression of so-called free people in certain nations. I understood, then, that freedom as we had it in the United States was not only rare, but sacred. It was worth dying for.

I made a commitment to myself upon arriving back in the United States that I would give something in return for all the privileges I had. I didn't know how, but I knew that as soon as I was settled, I would begin serving in some capacity to help strengthen the freedoms that I enjoyed. As I thought about it, I knew that I *owed* something to this country, to the people who had fought for its freedom, to its great leaders, and finally, to the Lord, because I came to know that the United States of America was not something that happened by chance; it was an act of providential design.

When I left the Navy in 1960 and settled in Salt Lake, I got a job selling insurance for John Hancock Mutual Life. This allowed me to support my family while I looked for ways to serve the community. I had graduated from the University of Utah in Banking and Finance, and, although I didn't have much experience, I thought I might use this where I could. I got involved in the Junior Chamber of Commerce and was soon put to work on a number of committees, some overseeing the expenditures of Chamber funds and others directly serving groups and individuals in the city. I *loved* the work we did. I could see how many people could be served by a group of good people engaged in good causes. I joined the Kiwanis Club and continued serving, working on a volunteer basis for individuals and groups who needed charitable assistance. As I served I found that I was benefitted every bit as much as those we helped. I felt myself growing and becoming more sure of myself, both as a citizen and as a husband and father.

During this time I discovered an important fact: members of the Church of Jesus Christ of Latter-day Saints need to be active members of the community. Church activity, though important, is not *all* that the Lord requires; we should give of ourselves on a broader basis, offering our time and talents to the country or city in which we live. I found that as I filled my Church duties, civic opportunities opened up for me. I also found that I had time for both.

Soon I discovered that I could do only so much in service clubs and the Chamber of Commerce. If I really wanted to become involved in the community, I had to get involved in the political process. The very nature of our government demands that change come through the elective process, a process that is not always easy or desirable. Although I had no plans of my own to run for office, I began to see that I could effect change through helping another good person, somebody I could trust and support, to gain elective office. I got involved in a friend's (Sherm Lloyd) campaign for Congress that year, 1960. We set up a movement called the Grass Rooters, and Sherm asked me to help run it. During that unfortunately unsuccessful campaign, I sought other ways to serve and was made a Republican Voting District Chairman, a Republican Legislative District Chairman, and was asked to serve on the State Finance Committee. I doubt very much that I was the best person available for these positions, but I was willing, and that distinguished me from many other more capable people. Over the next few years, I became involved in Senator Wallace Bennett's successful reelection campaign as well as a number of other campaigns for Congressmen, Senators, and local leaders. All of this gave me a great deal of experience, but until 1966 I didn't know what the experience might be used for.

I was flying for the Air National Guard then, and we were trying to negotiate a new lease for our land on the east side of the Salt Lake International Airport. We had been using the airport for years at a nominal charge, and in return we had spent hundreds of thousands of dollars in airport maintenance and improvements, including new taxi-ways, overlays of runways, providing fire-fighting equipment, and so on. The mayor and

City Commission were giving us headaches over the small fee we were paying; all they saw was what we were getting, not what we were giving in return. So they decided to raise the lease by a substantial amount. I was asked by my superiors in the Guard if I would join the negotiating group and see if I couldn't help the City to see our point and allow the existing lease to remain.

Now to be honest, I must admit to a rather large fault; I lose my temper sometimes. My mother has always warned me about it, and my wife and children have chastised me for it, but it's still there: I get mad and say things sometimes that I regret later. Fortunately this weakness has subsided somewhat in recent years, but in 1966 I still had it—in spades.

Our negotiating committee was meeting with City officials, still trying to get them to see the inequity of their position, and one particular Commissioner was really hard-headed. Of course, I availed him of this fact, in no uncertain terms, and he looked at me and said, "Captain Garn, if you don't like the way we run the city, why don't you run against me?" I stared right back at him and said, "Maybe I will. Any darn fool could run it better than you do." I was thirty-four years old, and with those words I embarked on a path that would change my life forever.

I initially dismissed the idea of actually running against him, but key people in the party kept badgering me about it, and after awhile I thought it might be a good idea myself. I didn't see how I could beat him, but I thought that the experience might be beneficial. Three months later I entered a field of nineteen candidates for two City Commission seats. We immediately conducted a poll to see how popular I was and found, to my sadness, that I had a two percent name identity city-wide. This was distressing, but perhaps what bothered me most was that on the east bench area, where I had grown up and gone to school, I only had a fifteen percent name identity. I thought that I had been more important than that in high school and college. Fifteen percent. I almost wanted to quit right there. But it was then that I learned the value of two-and-a-half-minute talks. I went door-to-door and gave hundreds of them, maybe thousands. And every time somebody drummed up a debate or a forum for the nineteen candidates to speak in, I only had about two-and-a-half minutes to talk in, and if I didn't get my views across then, I never did. I used up a lot of shoe leather. I ended up spending $3,500 in the campaign, which was all of the contributions I had received, and somehow ended up finishing first in the election.

So I was now a full-time City Commissioner, thanks to my hasty temper, and I had to learn a lot, fast. The Commission named me to be the new Water Commissioner, which meant, for those old enough to remember one of our great radio shows, that I was the Great Gildersleeve of Salt Lake City, the man who oversaw the city's water supply. Little did I dream, as I was growing up, that I would one day be the Great Gildersleeve of Salt Lake City.

As time went on, I found that as a City Commissioner I really didn't have the power to change things that I thought I could. I discovered that if I really wanted to change things, I needed to be mayor. So in the next election I ran for mayor and won. This allowed me to make some changes, but I found out soon enough that the mayor is only the local manager of the Federal Government in his city. If you *really* want to make changes, you have to go to Washington. So, in 1974 I ran for the United States Senate and won again. Now, I thought, I can really make changes.

All of my public service started because I wanted so badly to give something back to the country that had given me so much. Until those harsh words, "Any darn fool can run it better than you do," I had not entertained the idea of running for public office. And even then, despite my words, I didn't really see myself running for anything beyond city government. I wanted to be of help, as I had been in the Kiwanis Club and in the Junior Chamber of Commerce. I wanted to improve local situations within my scope of service. There's an old saying in Washington that "all politics are local." This generally refers to politicians covering their backsides back home—they vote not as their consciences tell them to but as their major supporters want them to. But since being in the Senate, I have learned that this is true in a different way. All service, whether performed on a national level or an international level, affects people back home. The good that is done in Washington or Dallas or San Francisco affects people in Salt Lake City. The good that is done in Moscow or Peking or New Delhi has a ripple effect and helps people living in Provo or Richfield or Kanab. All politics are local; they help—or hurt—people everywhere. With that in mind, I have tried to effect changes for good—wherever I have been.

Because I feel strongly about this, I feel great disappointment, almost anger, at the lack of participation of many citizens in the democratic processes of the government. Even fellow Saints sometimes become uninterested or jaded and refuse to do the simple things like voting. For whatever reason, they have forfeited their right, and their responsibility, to support the processes of freedom. Sometimes I wonder if they truly know what they have in the United States, that they are the beneficiaries of the blood, sweat and toil of countless others who preceded them.

I flew cargo missions to South Vietnam in the Sixties as a pilot in the Utah Air National Guard. On one of these trips I went into Saigon and spent some time among the people. I was introduced to a young woman on the street who had a little boy in a pushcart. He didn't have any hands or feet. I asked the woman if her boy had been accidentally injured in the war. She said no, that the injuries to her son had been intentional. The Viet Cong had told her that if she or her husband were seen at the polls on election day her son's feet and hands would be cut off. The Viet Cong had kept their promise. Another woman told me about her daughter being dipped in boiling water up to her waist for the same reason. I heard stories of mayors and local leaders being assassinated by the Viet Cong, and of voters being killed for going to the polls. Yet they participated. Eighty percent of the South Vietnamese voted in their elections. Eighty percent wanted freedom and democracy enough to vote for it, despite the risks. I came home from that trip shaken, angry and upset about the apathy of the American people.

Here, fifty percent of the people don't vote, and that's with no threats at all. How few of us would participate in the democratic process with the kinds of consequences suffered in Vietnam? I can't even say that I might have the courage if I knew that a child of mine would be mutilated. Our Founding Fathers risked their lives, their fortunes and their sacred honor, as the Preamble to the Declaration of Independence tells us, to give us our freedom. Can't we be participants in the political process that has given us more freedom, more opportunity, more material abundance than any of God's children have ever known? This process is sacred. We must preserve it. One of the most fundamental ways to do this is to vote.

The Viet Cong forced people to live a certain way. They threatened terror and mayhem if they didn't get their way. They killed and maimed if they were frustrated. There were two plans of government, one democratic and one communistic, and I know from whence they came. The latter-day scriptures reveal the source of coercion and intimidation, of a plan laid to force people to conform. They also reveal the source of freedom, of self-government, and of choice. I feel that by "choosing" in an election I am furthering the course of freedom, and thus I am supporting that eternal plan of free agency. I honestly feel that such an act is sacred.

There is no doubt in my mind that the Constitution is inspired. I know that God reserved this land to be a bastion of freedom, to be a new hope for the world, and I know that he used this freedom to restore his true gospel to the earth. Religious freedom requires political freedom. One might ask why the Lord didn't choose to restore his gospel to the earth in a European country. By 1830, some of the nations there were achieving democracy, and many of the fine people who would soon become Saints were already living there, both on the continent and in England. But democracy wasn't absolute yet. Most of these countries had state religions—the English Church or Lutheranism or Catholicism—religions were supported by the state. True free agency did not yet exist. Only in America were conditions right for such a movement. And even here the Church initially barely survived as the members were hounded from

New York to Pennsylvania to Ohio to Missouri to Illinois and finally to a remote Mexican territory without a name. Brigham named it Deseret, and it wasn't made a state until 1896 because of the tenets of the restored Church. It is humbling to consider that even the Constitution of the United States wasn't able, at first, to guarantee the religious freedoms required by the gospel of Jesus Christ, not through any weakness in the Constitution itself, but because of the interpretations and management of those holding elective offices. With this in mind, it becomes doubly important to participate in the electoral process.

When I was the mayor of Salt Lake I was a little disturbed by the fact that most of the boards and commissions were filled by nonmembers of the Church. I felt that perhaps as members of the Church we were a little apathetic. We want the Lord to bless us, and we want the government to help us, but we seem unwilling to dedicate a part of our lives to earning those blessings and help. Most of these nonmember public officials were good, honest individuals who had a lot to offer, but that didn't excuse the rest of us from offering our time in public service. Our prophets have always taught us that we have *double* the responsibilities of those outside the kingdom. They've taught that loyalty to the government is a basic part of the gospel. Consider our current Prophet, Ezra Taft Benson. He served diligently in the United States government for years, both before and after he was called as an Apostle. Let him be our model. Yes, we need to serve in the Church. Yes, we need to be with our families. But we also need to nurture the political processes wherever we live. We need to get up out of our chairs and find a worthy cause and go do something about it. We at least need to vote.

There are those out there who would take your freedoms from you if you let them. Many of them don't want to infringe on your rights, but they are so single-minded in their cause that they ignore the freedoms of others. I was mayor during a very turbulent time and had an opportunity to work with, and sometimes oppose, some of these people. The Sixties were difficult times for the country, and Salt Lake City was no exception. Various groups, most of them anti-war protestors, demonstrated in the streets of Salt Lake from time to time. I remember calling in the Police Chief and several of his key officers and telling them: "I'm grateful that these people live in a country where they can organize and demonstrate. I'm grateful that they have the right of free speech, whether I agree with them or not. But they *will* obey the law. They will stay on the sidewalks. They will observe traffic signs. They will not infringe on the rights of others." And sure enough the night after that first protest, I took some heat on the evening news. Demonstrators said that we were being too tough, that the police were forcing them to stay on the sidewalks, and that they weren't free to demonstrate as they pleased. Some of them came in personally and complained of police brutality, and I told them that I didn't believe the police had been out of line. I thought they were restrained in their control of the crowd, but that they *were* going to enforce the laws of the municipality. The protesters didn't like that. I told them that although I didn't support their position, I supported their right to protest, and that I would protect that right. But they needed to understand that the laws pertained to all people.

The next night they came in again, complaining that the police had used dogs on leashes to keep the protesters on the sidewalks. I said that police dogs are commonly used in crowd control and that the police, again, had been very judicious in their use of force. The protesters didn't like that. They wanted more rights than the rest of us have. The next night, they came into my office again, and this time I lost my temper.

I said: "Look, I'm getting a little tired of your complaints. Your people have broken laws and city ordinances every day, and we've been lenient. We've let you impose on other citizens' rights and generally make a nuisance of yourselves, but from now on if you don't behave yourselves I'll tell the police to let their dogs attack you. We'll do everything we can within the law to keep you in control." Of course the next day there were plenty of stories about mean Mayor Garn, but the march that day was orderly. They stayed where they were supposed to and generally conducted themselves quite well. They were able to protest within the law and still make their point. Their natural inclinations, though, as with many people, were to encroach on the freedoms of others and to bend the laws in their favor.

I don't believe that we will ever be free of that threat. In a democracy, everybody can have their say, and that makes for conflict. A conflict of words is one thing; a conflict of people and powers is something else. The best way for us to protect our peace *and* our freedoms is to be involved in the issues early, to educate ourselves and to exercise our right to vote.

One of the greatest lessons I've learned about democracy came in East Germany. We talk about voting and free speech, and although these are very important issues, they are nothing like the issues that citizens of the communist countries had to deal with for over forty years.

I was asked by our leaders to participate in arms-control negotiations with the Eastern Block countries in November, 1989. The meetings were scheduled to be held in Vienna and Geneva, but when the Berlin Wall began to open up we diverted our group there and made it a fact-finding trip. We went immediately to Berlin, which, at that time was a divided city surrounded by communist East Germany. My wife, Kathleen, was able to accompany me on the trip. Although the Berlin Wall had opened up two weeks earlier, very little had changed between the two sections of the city. Checkpoint Charley, the gate between East and West Berlin, was still monitored by State police, with one-day visas being granted for East Germans to enter West Berlin. As we approached Checkpoint Charley from the west, we saw large crowds gathered along the wall, and I asked the driver to stop the car. The air was filled with hammering and chinking noises as these people tried to break sections of the wall down. It was an impressive sight. The wall itself is huge. By comparison it would absolutely dwarf the wall around Temple Square in Salt Lake City. Chips were flying off, and the noise was almost like orchestrated music, with pounding and clinking and chipping coming from the full length. I walked over to a group using chisels and hammers. One of the young men was an American, and I asked him how he was able to do this with East German guards, some carrying machine guns, still sitting in their towers watching. He said that technically we weren't even supposed to approach the wall, that it was set about ten or fifteen feet back on East German soil. We were standing in "No Man's Land." So I asked him how they were getting away with it, and he said, "Oh, the guards come down about every hour or so and confiscate our tools." I looked up at the guards sitting in their towers.

"If the guards take your tools," I asked, "how do you get them back?"

"They sell them back to us."

I smiled. "Capitalism already."

"Capitalism already," he agreed. Then he showed me an East German guard hat. "In fact, I bought this too."

I was impressed. The wall was coming down, and people who had never known freedom were already taking advantage of it. The young American said that he and his friends were selling these chips to finance a trip around Europe. He offered me one, and I asked how much. He eyed me more carefully and said, "You look familiar."

"No," I said, "I don't think we know each other."

"Where are you from, Ohio?"

"No."

"I've seen you somewhere before."

"I really don't think we know . . ."

"Oh yeah! You flew in space. You're one of those astronauts—and a senator."

"You're right."

"Here, you deserve one free," and he handed me his hammer and chisel so that I could break off some pieces of the Berlin Wall myself.

I got back in the car, and we proceeded through Checkpoint Charley and into East Berlin. I was amazed by the line of people, three or four abreast, waiting to be given permission to enter West Berlin. The line was perhaps two miles long. Many of these people had family or friends in West Berlin that they hadn't seen in decades. Patiently, anxiously, they waited for their first chance ever to visit a true democracy, a land where they would be allowed to walk where they pleased, say what they wanted, and actually participate, with their small means, in a free market. As we drove through town I saw evidences of an oppressed people. Most of the buildings were gray, and many were dilapidated. Rubble still lay in vacant lots from World War II. The streets almost seemed vacated. Little cars called *Travants* came down the road periodically, impossibly small and powered, at best, by lawn-mower-sized engines. Street lighting was almost nonexistent, just a bare bulb here and there. People on the streets wore drab clothing and much of it ill-fitting, at least by our standards. The people themselves seemed dour, dejected. The vibrancy I had felt just a few hundred yards away in the West was nowhere to be seen. The very spirit was different. The city seemed to be living a gray existence—black and white.

I tried to imagine a wall being run through Salt Lake City, separating the city in half, making one side free and the other ruled by a dictator for forty years. I couldn't visualize it. I couldn't see one half of the valley lying in rubble, emotionally and temporally, and the other operating as it always has, with energy and motivation. Something terrible had happened in this land of brilliant engineers, mathematicians, architects, artists, musicians, and the like. Half of Germany, home to some of the world's greatest talent, was almost forty years behind the times. I was seeing the effects of a living tragedy, and my heart ached for the loss.

Kathleen and I went to a dinner that night at the American Ambassador's home in East Germany. He had invited members of the East German *Politburo*, as well as members of the New Forum, and other dissidents, who, until recently, would have been considered enemies of the State. This was actually a rather daring thing for the Ambassador to do, and some of the people there were unsure of what to expect.

As the dinner got under way, Kathleen was seated next to one of the young dissidents who spoke a little English. When a plate was brought out, filled with steak filets with wrapped bacon, his eyes grew large. Kathleen was given a larger steak than he was, and she offered to exchange it with him. He quickly accepted. During the meal, she told him that she couldn't finish the steak on her plate and asked him if he would like it too. He said, "I don't want to be rude, Mrs. Garn, but I really would. I've never had a steak before." The room was decorated exquisitely, and the table was adorned with large centerpieces of flowers and fruit and was set with the finest china and silver. After the meal, this young man turned to Kathleen and said, "Mrs. Garn, I'm an educated man, and I'm a little embarrassed, but would you mind if I eat the centerpiece? We just don't have fruit like that."

All of us from the West were hearing stories like this. A young woman sitting on my left was a journalist in East Germany. She had been hired by the Associated Press to write stories on the breakup of the Eastern governments and the destruction of the wall. She said, "Do you know how much they pay me, Senator?" And I said, no, how much? "Five hundred dollars. Do you know how much five hundred dollars is? My family will have to be very careful and very wise in how we spend it. I have never seen five hundred dollars before."

The man on my right was a Ph.D. in biology, who was also part of the New Forum, a new group of leaders and thinkers who wanted to take the country into democracy. I will never forget my conversation with him.

"I understand that you went to my church this morning," he said.

I told him that was true, that I had visited the Lutheran Church there in East Berlin.

"That is where our movement started," he said. "That is where we gave each other support and exchanged ideas. We need democracy."

He seemed troubled by something then and finally said, "I will tell you something very embarrassing. I have been working on a project in microbiology for fifteen years—ever since getting my Ph.D. I am forty years old now. A couple of weeks ago, when the wall opened up, I got some information. I found out that the work I am doing was discovered more than twenty years ago in your country. My government would not let me read any literature from the West for fear of contaminating me. I have, how you say, reinvented the wheel."

I saw the sadness in his face, the knowledge written there that he had wasted the last fifteen years of his professional life. I asked him to tell me more about himself.

"When I was seventeen," he said, "my father and I walked out of that Lutheran church you were in today, and a group of people were waiting for us. We thought they were friends. My father made a very mild anti-government statement, and we went on. Shortly afterwards, the Secret Police came and picked him up, and we didn't know what happened to him. For thirteen years we didn't know if he had been killed or was imprisoned or was being tortured. He was just gone, and we could get no information. One day thirteen years later he was returned home, a broken, tired, sick old man who would never be the same again.

"Yesterday, I saw my twenty-one-year-old daughter for the first time in seven years."

"Where has she been?" I asked.

"Seven years ago, we were lucky enough to be able to smuggle her to West Berlin. We put her under the floor boards of a car and got her past the guards." He stopped speaking for a moment and lowered his head. When he looked back at me there were tears in his eyes. "Do you know how hard it is to choose whether you give your daughter freedom or whether you raise her?"

I said I didn't. "I have seven children, and I don't know what I would do if faced with that choice."

"Losing our daughter has been the most agonizing thing we have ever done. But we have two other children, and we have been looking for ways to get them out, too. Freedom is worth all that we have."

I couldn't speak. A moment later he continued. "Our daughter doesn't dare come back home. She's afraid for her life here. So we hope that we will have that wall torn down in five years. Maybe then she can come home, and we can be a family again. A free family."

The dinner was continuing as before, most people visiting with their neighbors rather than eating. My friend was sitting silently now, perhaps considering his family at home.

"How can you sacrifice so much for freedom?" I asked. "You're forty years old. You've lived under communism your entire life. How can you feel so strongly about something you've never known?"

"Senator," he said, "you don't understand. Freedom is inborn. God gave us freedom. The Communists have imprisoned my body for forty years, but they have not imprisoned my soul."

I felt that for the first time, perhaps, I really did understand freedom.

Kathleen came over after a while and asked what was wrong with me. She said, "I've been watching you cry all evening." I said, "I've been watching you cry all evening, too, so don't give me any of that business." And it turned out that most of the Westerners there were hearing similar stories, stories that melted our hearts and gave us renewed gratitude for the privileges we had always known.

The next day we reentered East Berlin to visit the spot where the Peace Treaty was signed that ended World War II. This was where the Germans, Americans, and the Russians had ended that most terrible of wars. Before we got to the spot, we were stopped by a line of people holding hands and singing. The line seemed to extend in both directions as far as we could see. A policeman came over to our bus and explained that people all across East Germany were holding hands for twenty minutes. "We'll let them do it for twenty minutes," he said, "but no longer." We got out of the bus and went up to the people. They claimed that the line extended through East Germany, from border to border, all the people clasping hands in a show of unity. This was their way of demonstrating peaceably. We all got into the line and held hands and joined with them for fifteen or twenty minutes in one of the most emotional expressions of unity and hope I have ever seen. We couldn't sing their songs, but we felt their hearts, and we were honored to be with them. I don't think there was a dry eye or an untouched heart from one border to the other.

I came home from Germany a changed man. Kathleen and I gathered our children together and shared what we had seen and heard. We expressed our love for our children and for the freedoms we have, and then we told them that we didn't want to hear them complain about little things they didn't have. I told them that I'd take them to East Germany if they did, and then they could see what other children were living like.

Of course, it's not called East Germany anymore. The wall came down far quicker than anybody thought it would, certainly quicker than the five years that my friend in East Berlin anticipated. The country is reunified, and the people now, from border to border, share a unity much stronger than handclasps. They share a unity of heart, of spirit. They are finally free.

Free agency is a gift of God, but it must be earned. Just as our Savior battled forces to guarantee us the freedom to work out our own salvation, men and women have died that freedom might be guaranteed in our homes and countries. What are we doing to guarantee that freedom for others—for our own children?

The United States is not an accident. There is nothing like it, and there never has been. It allows people like sheltered young boys from Utah to go to Washington and make a difference in national and international policy. It allows people to raise their voices, to be heard, to make choices, to decide for themselves how to conduct their lives. I believe that we will find, when we have passed on and are on the other side, that those of us who lived in this land had a special responsibility to maintain the rights and privileges granted in the Constitution; and that those of us in the Church, as our Prophets have told us, had the double responsibility of supporting both the Restored Church *and* the elective process of democracy. Our charge is to be active in both venues, spiritually and temporally. Our charge is to make a difference for good. I have the strongest conviction that the Lord will bless us as we help ourselves, and that he is anxiously watching over us, waiting for us to grow in our free agency. The opportunity is ours.

My mother, Agnes Fern Christensen.
(Photo courtesy Jake Garn.)

My father, Jacob Edwin Garn.
(Photo courtesy Jake Garn.)

. . . In the Power of
the Priesthood

People have called me a skeptic over the years. They know that I prefer tangible evidence in the decisions I make and that I am a stickler for taking pragmatic positions. Sometimes while listening to a talk in sacrament meeting, I'll look for logical or scientific evidence to back up a "faith-promoting" story. I don't like believing just for the sake of believing. But there are times, and every person with a testimony knows this, that powers beyond our own intervene in our lives. There are times when the unmistakable power of the priesthood blesses us beyond anything we can do ourselves. It is because of these blessings, and because of the sweet, peaceful influence of the Spirit afterwards, that I know that God acts in our behalf through the priesthood.

In Section 46 of the Doctrine and Covenants the Lord tells us that some have "faith to be healed," and others have "faith to heal." Over the years I have come to the conclusion that all worthy priesthood holders can have the gift of healing if they magnify their callings and exercise faith. This may sound strange to people outside the Church, and even to some in it, but I have seen this gift expressed too many times, both in my own life and in the lives of others, to deny it. The Lord says that when we do what he says that he is bound. When we are righteous, the powers of heaven will rest upon us and we will be able to exercise the various gifts of priesthood power as they are necessary for us.

As a young man I had been called upon to give priesthood blessings, sometimes in the capacity of a home teacher or to family members, but I never knew that I had made a difference. Being the skeptic that I am, I doubted that the Lord had heard the blessing or that the power of the priesthood had really been exercised on those occasions. I don't know if I lacked faith or if I was just insensitive to the Spirit. Then came an experience which made me believe. Afterwards, I knew that the power of the Lord was there, just waiting for us to use it in faith.

Our daughter, Susan, was born while I was still in the Service in Oak Harbor, Washington. She was our second child, and as our first daughter, she was a real blessing to the family. Just before she was to come home from the hospital, she developed a staph infection in her chest and left side. The doctors began treating her with an antibiotic, but the infection resisted it, and the doctors changed prescriptions. The infection resisted this too, and all the other antibiotics available, and soon her temperature rose to a critical level. Her sores became inflamed, and it was obvious that she was in a lot of pain. There is nothing more frustrating than watching your child suffer while you can do nothing about it. Because of the contagious nature of her illness, no one except the doctors and ourselves were allowed in the room, and we had to put on masks, robes, and gloves before entering.

A new strain of antibiotics was available nearby in Seattle, and I called a good friend of mine who lived there to pick up a prescription for it at the hospital and bring it down, which he did. Our hopes were riding on this new medicine. We prayed that the Lord would bless our daughter, that the medicine would work and she would recover. That night, it became obvious that the medicine was not having any effect on her, and she became weaker. The bishop came over and asked if he could give her a blessing, but the doctors refused to let him in the room. My wife, Hazel, looked at me and asked what we should do, and I knew that I only had one choice; I said that I was going in there to give our daughter a blessing. Hazel asked if it didn't take two people to do it, and I told her that under the circumstances I thought the Lord would understand. So I put on the robe and gloves and mask and went into the room and anointed her with oil. Then I sealed the anointing and gave her a blessing of strength. As I said these words, I felt the Spirit resting upon me, filling me with a peace that I had not felt before. Hazel and I went home and prayed again before going to bed.

The next morning we found the doctor at Susan's side. The fever had broken and she was much stronger. He just marvelled and said, "Boy, I had no idea the antibiotics would work that fast." I looked at him and said, "I don't think they did, Doctor," and Hazel and I just looked at each other. We went to our daughter's bed and saw a happy, peaceful baby. There was no doubt that the Lord had blessed her. We knew that without the power of the priesthood she might not have recovered. This was the first time that I felt the Spirit direct me in a blessing, and as a result, my faith grew stronger. I knew that the Lord would be with me—that he would be bound—if I did his will.

81

There are times when the power of the priesthood works hand in hand with the procedures of modern medicine. There are times, such as when Hazel was diagnosed with breast cancer, that both powers are invoked. I feel that we are under obligation to use the resources the Lord has made available through learning and study as well as those available through faith.

Hazel had just turned thirty when she was diagnosed with breast cancer at her six-week checkup after the birth of our son, Jeff. This was in the mid-Sixties, and the treatment for cancer was not nearly as developed, or effective, as it is now. The prognosis was not good. They were afraid that the cancer had spread to the lymph nodes and surrounding muscles and that it was just a matter of time before it spread to other areas of the body. Before she was admitted to the hospital the children and I knelt with her in a family circle and prayed for the Lord to bless her. We were all scared and knew that we needed the help of the Lord. Then I gave her the first of many priesthood blessings, promising her that the Lord would be with her and would bless her according to our faith and prayers.

She had a radical mastectomy, which means that the entire breast was removed, along with the lymph nodes and surrounding muscles in the shoulder and arm. The operation went fine, but she was very weak afterwards. The doctors weren't sure if the cancer had all been removed or not. Only time would tell.

These became difficult days for me. As I pondered the possibility of losing my wife—of our four children losing their mother—I wondered why this had happened to us. I even wondered if the Lord had *done* it to us, and if so, why? She was a wonderful woman, devoted to her family, and we were all active in the Church--what more could we have done? I wondered if the Lord was punishing us for something, but I couldn't figure out what it was. And as these thoughts entered my mind, I became upset and more confused. Finally, it was Hazel who straightened me out.

It was several weeks after the surgery, and I was moping around worrying about things, and she said, "Jake, I just don't understand you. You're grumpy and depressed and worrying about me; if I remember right, it was I who had the mastectomy, not you. Shape up. I don't like living with somebody that's as sad and obnoxious as you." It was like a slap on the face, and it woke me up. She had great faith, much greater than mine, and she knew that everything would be all right. She told me repeatedly that she knew she would not die of cancer and that she would be of great help to others. Shortly afterwards, this began to be fulfilled.

Another sister in our ward also had breast cancer and had gone through a mastectomy a couple weeks after Hazel did. During her recovery she became very depressed. Much of the danger of mastectomies is the emotional trauma that the patient can suffer afterwards. If it's not treated right and diffused, it can prove to be more damaging than the original cancer. Hazel and I went over to the sister's house and visited with her. She was very kind, but after a while it became apparent that words alone weren't going to help her. Hazel then held up her blouse and showed the sister the bandages all the way down her body. The stitches were still there and the muscles around the shoulder were gone. Then Hazel expressed her joy at being alive and still having the opportunity to raise her children and be with her husband. This made an impression on the sister, who suddenly realized that many women had this type of surgery and that there really was hope for her.

83

As Hazel continued in her recovery, the doctors were impressed. Although she had difficulty using her arm because of the muscles missing, she displayed a remarkably positive attitude and seemed to be making great progress. Once, when she was experiencing weakness and more pain in her shoulder, we had the bishopric come over and we gave her a blessing. She regained her strength soon after, and the pain subsided. During all of this, she remained convinced that the cancer would not take her from her family.

As she grew stronger, she visited other women in hospitals who had gone through the same or similar surgeries. Sometimes she took me along "because sometimes husbands aren't very understanding." Once, we visited a woman who had lost a breast, and she was having more trouble with her husband than with the surgery. This sounded familiar. As I had been, he was afraid of losing his wife and was worried about the family. When Hazel tried to talk to them about the woman's recovery and how to deal with the emotions that they felt, the husband became upset. He asked her what right she had to come into the hospital and tell people how to deal with their emotions when she hadn't gone through it herself. His wife just said, "Shut up, Henry. She's had a mastectomy herself. She knows all about it." He was very embarrassed and asked Hazel's forgiveness. Because of her prosthesis, he hadn't been able to tell that she too had had the operation. Hazel went on to become the first leader in Utah for the American Cancer Society's "Reach to Recovery Program." In that capacity she literally fulfilled the promise that she had felt from the Spirit earlier, that she would become a great help to others as a result of her illness.

Doctors generally feel that if a breast-cancer patient can go five years without a recurrence that she is cured. As we neared that time frame, Hazel often told me that I should have had more faith, that there really hadn't been anything to worry about. By the time we reached ten years, I started to believe her. She was healed. Throughout the remainder of her life she would never again know the vestiges of cancer.

I could never say that the priesthood blessings alone healed her, just as I could never say that modern medicine alone healed her. The Lord blessed all involved; he blessed the doctors and the medicines and the faith of our family and all those who prayed for her, and most importantly, he blessed *her*. He blessed her spiritually and physically. She was a better person after her experience, and our family was blessed by the strength she brought to it. My love and respect for her grew, and I realized how delicate my own faith was. I knew that my faith in the Lord and his priesthood needed to grow. With time, it would have ample opportunity to do just that.

Our youngest child, Jennifer, once gave us more than enough reason to exercise our faith. I can't honestly say that it was the type of reason we wished for, but when the time came, we were grateful for the priesthood.

Senator Howard Baker, of Tennessee, had invited Kathleen and me to a reception at his home one evening. We were new parents again with the recent birth of Jennifer, and we tried to beg out of it by saying that we needed to stay home with the baby. As was usual for him, though, he was undeterred.

"Oh, Jake," he said, "at your age we ought to be showing *you* off at the reception. You'd better come, and you'd better bring that wife and baby of yours."

Now, I didn't think that forty-nine was so old to be a father again, but I went along with him anyway and told him that we'd be there. On the night of the reception, I came home from the

Capitol to pick Kathleen and Jennifer up, and found Kathleen in tears, holding the baby. I knew immediately that something was wrong. Kathleen said the doctor was waiting for us, so we jumped into the car and sped to his office.

Kathleen had gotten ready for the reception and was carrying Jennifer in a plastic baby carrier down the stairs. On the landing, halfway down, one of the other children had left a toy, and Kathleen stepped on it, causing her to fall down the rest of the stairs. The baby had flown out of the carrier and landed head-first on the tile floor at the bottom. Immediately, the left side of her head began to swell up, and when I got there, the hematoma had swollen so large that the side of her head was pressing down on her ear, nearly covering it. As soon as we got to the office, the doctor came out and looked at her. He told us to get back in the car and take her to the hospital, where he would meet us. There was little he could do for us at the office, he said. He went back inside and called ahead, directing the X-ray staff and a neurosurgeon to be ready to receive her.

When we got to the hospital, the X-ray technician took her right in and began preparing her for a chest X-ray. I asked him what he was doing, and he said that it was standard procedure for all children to be given chest X-rays when they came in. I couldn't believe it.

"Would you look at her head?" I said. "She might be dying, and you want to X-ray her chest?"

"We have to."

"I don't care what you have to do, you X-ray her head right now!"

He looked at me a moment then decided to X-ray her head. He got out a vice and started to put her head in it.

"What are doing?" I asked.

86

"I've got to put her head in this vice to keep it still."

"You can't put my baby's head a vice!" I moved over to him. "Here, I'll hold her head and you take the X-ray."

"I can't, your hand will get in the way."

I gently took Jennifer's head in my hands. "Look, I'll put my fingers around her head this way, on the other side, and you can take a picture of the area where the swelling is."

"But your fingers will get X-rayed."

"I really don't care if my fingers get X-rayed. This is what we're going to do."

"I don't know—"

"Do it, now!"

He went around the panel and took the picture. I have found that the imperative voice can be an excellent motivation for some people.

After the X-rays were taken, they wheeled Jennifer into another room and connected her to various monitors. The neurosurgeon arrived and took a look at the X-rays. Without seeing Jennifer first, he said, "Well, I really don't see anything wrong. On the X-rays she looks fine." Then he came in and took a look at her. Suddenly he wasn't sure about the X-rays after seeing the massive swelling, and he decided that he'd better take one more look at them. When he came back, he apologized and said that he had somehow missed a hairline fracture of her skull from the soft spot in the top of her head all the way down to her ear. Her head was literally cracked all the way on one side. After examining her closer, he said that he couldn't find any swelling in the brain, that most of it was exterior, and that there wasn't much we could do except wait. It might take a few days, he said, or it might take a few weeks. Fortunately, he didn't think that there was any brain damage.

It was now after one a.m., and our family physician had been with us the whole time. I walked over and said to him, "Doctor Horne, what are you still doing here?"

"Well, Senator," he said, "I just figured that you and your wife might need me. In fact, you know that there's no way that your wife is going to leave here tonight. Why don't you go home and get whatever she needs, clothes, toothbrush, whatever, and I'll stay with her until you get back."

I think that is when I fell in love with our doctor, the man who would later become my son-in-law. I didn't know that he would play such a large part in our lives, but I knew then that there were very few people in the world like him. After I had come back, and sent Doctor Horne home, I asked the nurses if Kathleen and I could have a few minutes alone with our child. I didn't have any consecrated oil, but I put my hands on her head and gave her a priesthood blessing. Again, I felt a calm presence come into me, and I felt that everything would be all right. Afterwards, we sat down, and sometime that night we both fell asleep.

Early the next morning, the doctor came in and looked at her. He was amazed. The swelling was virtually gone. Jennifer was doing fine, and all indications were that she was rapidly healing. Although we knew that the Lord was doing this, even we were a little amazed. It wasn't long before Jennifer was home and playing as if nothing had happened.

These are the moments when you *know* that God loves his children. This is when you know that he is aware of you, personally, and that he is anxious to bless you. When he restores your child to health, and he blesses you and your wife with a deep and abiding peace, you doubt no longer. You know.

A few years later, we had another scare with Jennifer. Because of the injury she had suffered to her head, we were always concerned when anything came up that seemed to be related to it. One night she had a fever that wouldn't go away; in fact, it was getting worse. Kathleen took her out of her crib and put her in the bed between us and tried to comfort her. It seemed like the little girl was just burning up. I put my hand on her head and couldn't believe how hot she was. So, in the middle of the night sometime, I got up, turned the light on, and got some consecrated oil. I didn't have another Melchizedek Priesthood holder to assist me, so I anointed her myself and began to seal the anointing. As I gave the blessing, I felt her head suddenly get cooler under my hands. It was one of the most dramatic sensations I have ever felt. I finished the blessing and just stood back. She was healed. The calm influence of the Spirit was there, and I knew, once again, that the Lord had intervened in our lives. He had answered the faith and simple prayer of a little girl's parents.

I am absolutely convinced that when a priesthood holder magnifies his callings the Lord will bless him with the gift of healing as he needs it. The most spiritual experiences of my life have come in these intimate moments, when the Lord has granted me the power to bless and heal my loved ones. I know that the Lord delights in honoring us as we honor him. But the burden is on us; we must obey his commandments and honor his priesthood. We must be prepared—and sometimes that is what keeps me towing the line. I don't dare give in to temptation for fear of being unworthy to bless my family. I don't believe that we can idly go along in our lives, disregarding the gospel, then ask the Lord for help when we need it. If we want him to be bound, then we must be bound. If we want his blessings, then we must live worthy of them. Although I view the gift of healing as sacred, and I hesitate to use it unnecessarily, I seek to be worthy of it at all times. I want to lead my life such that the Lord will be pleased to honor me when I exercise his priesthood in another's behalf.

Few people have the opportunity to give part of their very *selves* to save the life of a family member. We talk about giving of ourselves, but rarely do we face the challenge of sacrificing a part of our own life for the life of another. I was blessed to offer such a gift.

When Sue was ten years old we noticed her becoming progressively weaker. She began to tire easily, and we noticed that she was drinking a lot of water. At first we thought that she had the flu or a cold, but it continued to worsen, with signs of something more serious becoming apparent. I was at my office when I got a call from Hazel. She said to come immediately to Primary Children's Hospital. I asked her what was wrong with Sue, and she said that Sue had just been to the doctor's and was diagnosed with diabetes and that the doctors were so concerned about her that they were sending her to the hospital. I rushed to the hospital, not really knowing what to expect or even what, exactly, had happened. Like most people, I knew very little about diabetes.

When I arrived, I found my daughter just being wheeled into the hospital. I went first to her and my wife then to the front desk to check her in. Because of past experiences in taking my parents to the hospital, I knew the standard procedure—you always fill out your insurance information and other paperwork before being admitted into the hospital. This was before I had really gotten into politics and had become recognizable; I was a City Commissioner at the time, and I don't think *anybody* knows who they are. So I was surprised when the lady at the front desk looked at me and said, "Mr. Garn, don't you think you ought to be with your daughter?" I said, "Well, yes, I do, but don't I need to fill these forms out first?" She said, "Oh, do that later, maybe tomorrow. Right now, go be with your daughter." I was so impressed with this kindness that I made a mental note to repay it any way I could in the future.

We went in and found that Sue's diabetes was severe enough that it would require daily insulin shots. This meant that we had to learn how to administer the shots and how to regulate her diet so that her system had as little stress as possible. We learned that diabetes is the third largest killer in the country, and that there is no cure for it.

Both Sue and her mother practiced using a syringe by injecting water into an orange. As they were doing this in the hospital room, a nurse came by and saw what they were doing. "Oh, an orange doesn't really feel like skin," she said. "Here, you can practice on me." Hazel and Sue couldn't believe it. The nurse promptly offered her arm and the girls each gave her a shot. We received this kind of consideration, really going beyond the call of duty, all the way through our stay there. When the moment of truth came, though, when we got home, neither wanted to give the shot. They went back and forth, trying to decide who was going to do it, and I got so perturbed that I finally said, "Here, I'll do it." And I took the syringe and without any practice at all gave her the shot. The shot was fine, but I soon learned that I had made a big mistake. When the time came for her second shot, only one person was nominated—Dad. When the next shot came around, again, only Dad could do it. This became my job for the next four or five years.

I'll never forget my first trip away from home; it was a Utah Air Guard trip, and Sue was scared of somebody else having to give her the shot. Her mother had done it before, but Sue said that her shots hurt and that mine didn't. (Of course, the only reason my shots didn't hurt is because I didn't try to be careful. I just jabbed the needle in and took it out; her mother had a harder time being so ruthless.) But Sue eventually learned to give her own shots, and that took care of the problem; but for a few years there I rued that first shot.

As long as Sue maintained her diet and took her shots regularly, she was fine. She could do anything that other kids did, except, of course, indulge in rich desserts and sugary foods. This presented a problem sometimes. There is a tendency in most newly diagnosed diabetics to deny their illness. Sue was no different. She wanted to fit in with her friends, do what they did and eat what they ate, pretending that she was as healthy as everybody else. Diabetics often want to hide the disease, even from themselves, which can result in them being rushed into the emergency room in a diabetic coma. We went through this a few times before Sue fully realized the scope of her condition.

The side effects of diabetes are kidney failure, heart disease, restricted blood flow, loss of sight, and other related complications. As she matured and became more conscious of these potential problems, her condition leveled off. After a few years, though, she began to show signs of deterioration. She began laser treatments to stop blood vessels from bursting in her eyes, but the treatment was unsuccessful and one eye suddenly suffered a massive hemorrhage, causing total blindness in that eye. This scared all of us and made us more determined to protect her. She went to the hospital often to have her kidneys tested for decreased function, and the results were agonizingly consistent;

they too were gradually getting worse. No matter how faithful she was to doctors' orders, she couldn't stop her body from betraying her—especially her kidneys, which were slowly failing.

She had already received many priesthood blessings, and now our faith and prayers never left her. We knew that with the Lord's help she could be strengthened to endure all this, but we wanted a more permanent solution. We wanted her to enjoy a full and rich life, no matter the sacrifice or inconvenience. We were willing to pay whatever price was necessary to provide her this blessing. The Lord must have heard our prayers because a more permanent solution would soon become available.

In the middle of my third Senate campaign, in 1986, I was called home from a tour of the state. Sue's kidneys had almost completely failed her, and she was close to going in the hospital to start dialysis treatments to cleanse her blood. Her situation was very serious, and everybody in the family immediately offered to be a donor for a kidney transplant. Of course we all needed to be tested to see if any of us were suitable. Her brother Jeff was even tested in London while serving on his mission. We began having the tests at the University of Utah Medical Center, with each of us hoping that we would be the only one suitable. I remember coming out from one of these tests and a reporter approached me. I don't remember who he was, but I'll never forget his question: "Senator Garn, why would you do something like this?" I don't think I have ever been more baffled by the press. I was simply amazed by his ignorance. I said, "She's my daughter; that's why I would do this." He didn't seem to understand that this was a great privilege for me, that if I could stop my daughter from suffering simply by giving up one of my kidneys, I'd consider it an honor. I told him that I had always envied mothers a little, that they had the opportunity to create and bear life, that they could work in partnership with God and give part of themselves in giving life to another. Now, in a much smaller way, I could assist in lending life to my daughter.

Three of us in the family were half matches. That meant that we had half the genes necessary to completely match her gene structure and be a compatible donor. Since I was one of these, I told the others that I would be the donor. The children said that I wasn't being fair, but I explained, delicately, that I was the boss, and that was final. Of course, there were two other important reasons for my being the donor. One, I was the father, and I couldn't bear having two of my children on the operating table at the same time, and two, I wouldn't need my kidney nearly as long as the rest of them would. One of my children said, "Well, *you'll* be on the operating table, Dad." I replied, "I know, but I'll be asleep, so I won't have any idea what's going on." So, despite their protests, I became the nominee. But the process didn't end so easily. The doctors had two major concerns—me being only a half-match, and my age. I was fifty-four at the time, and they would prefer a younger donor. Putting the kidney in the recipient is only half the problem, taking it out of the donor and leaving him or her healthy is the other half. They began giving me batteries of tests that quickly became very tedious. I went through blood checks, and X-rays, and an arteriogram, in which they ran dye through my veins then took more X-rays of me, and so on. And it became very aggravating because I could see my daughter getting sicker every day and the doctors not coming any closer to an answer. After weeks of this, I began to despair. Every time I thought I would get the go-ahead, more concerns came up, and everything was put on hold. Then I received a blessing.

I was at Jon Huntsman's house, a long-time friend, and he was visiting with Elders David B. Haight and M. Russell Ballard. During the evening, I expressed my frustration with the doctors and my very real concern for the life of my daughter. Elder Haight then offered to give me a blessing. The other men all joined with him in laying their hands on my head and invoking the blessings of the holy priesthood. He told me that the Lord was watching over us, that the doctors would yet allow me to be the donor, and that the transplant would be a full success. It was a very powerful and emotional blessing, and from that moment I began to feel peace. The next morning at eight o'clock the hospital called and said that I had been cleared to be the donor.

There had been no change in the test results. There had been no new information during the night. The doctors had simply gotten together that morning and agreed to make me the donor. I knew, even if they didn't, that they had been helped in their decision. After the phone call, I cried. I wasn't sad, and I wasn't scared, I just felt utter relief that our prayers had finally been answered, that after the long weeks of anxiety and concern, and after a blessing from an Apostle of the Lord, the way had finally been cleared for me to help my daughter.

The night before the surgery our bishop in Washington DC, Frank Madsen, came over and assisted me in giving Sue another blessing. His blessing was truly inspirational. He promised both of us that we would have peace of mind. He also told us that the doctors would make all the correct decisions and be at the peak of their skills, and that the surgeries would be completely successful. He said that the Lord would watch over us and return us to our families and that our Heavenly Father would comfort our families while we were in surgery. Again, peace and calm came upon me, and I felt that all would be well. Because of these blessings, and because of the continued peace I felt, I knew that we would both be watched over by the Lord and recover fully.

Another visitor also surprised me that evening. I had just checked into the hospital there in Washington and was waiting in my room—beginning to feel a little anxious again—when Jon Huntsman showed up again. The blessing that I had received from him and Elders Haight and Ballard had been given at Jon's home in Salt Lake. Now here he was a few days later in Washington.

"What are you doing here?" I asked.

"Well," he said, "Karen and I were having breakfast this morning, and it just occurred to us that Kathleen would be alone all day long while you and Sue were in surgery. I just thought I'd come back and be with her."

I was deeply touched. He had changed his plans for those two days and flown to Washington when he realized that my wife would be alone. The love of this good friend again brought peace to me, and I was able to relax and sleep without concern through the night. The next day he would spend over twelve hours with Kathleen, taking her on walks and treating her to lunch. That meant more to me than I can ever tell him.

The next morning my daughter and I were on operating tables. The surgery on the donor is much more extensive than it is on the recipient. In my case, the doctors had to make an incision fifteen inches long, all the way around my side and up my back. They removed my tenth rib and cut the vertical muscles all along the side and back. I was literally laid open from one side to the other. My daughter, though, simply received an incision about the size of a C-Section and had the kidney placed in through that. The doctors didn't remove her other kidneys; they just laid the new one under the soft tissue on the right front side of her abdomen and attached it to the body. Within seconds her new kidney was operating fully. There was no lapse, no anxious moments, the kidney began to work like it had been there all along. They closed her up, and for the first time in years she had a fully functioning kidney.

When we came out of the anesthesia, they wheeled us into different rooms and let us spend the night resting. I called her on the hospital phone that evening, though, and asked her how she was doing. She sounded great. Just by the strength in her voice I could tell that she was doing better already. Her body was already healing itself, and the new kidney was ridding her body of all the wastes that had built up over the last few weeks. She asked how I was doing, and I had to tell her that I could hardly move. I didn't know pain like that was possible. When nurses or visitors came in, I had to ask them not to say anything funny because the slightest movement, even a giggle, put me in almost unbearable pain. The doctors had told me before the operation that they were going to make me feel miserable. They said: "Your daughter is sick, and we're going to make her feel better. You're healthy, and we're going to make you feel miserable." And they were right. I had a fever right after the operation, and for a while I thought that anything would be preferable to the pain I was experiencing in my body. It was several weeks before I began feeling totally normal again. Although my recovery was quicker than many kidney donors experience, it still seemed to take forever. Sue used to call me in the evenings (she was living in Washington, and I was back in Utah) and ask how I was doing. It seemed from her voice that she, too, was still feeling weak. I told her to hang in there and that she would eventually get better. I told her about the regimen of exercises the doctors had given me to do everyday and that I knew I would eventually feel better. A week or so later I flew back to Washington and was able to see her. To my surprise, she looked great. I was still moving like an old man, but she looked fitter than she had in years. Soon after I got there she said, "Dad, I feel guilty. I've been lying to you for weeks. I just pretended to be feeling bad so you wouldn't feel alone. I could tell that you were still in pain, and I felt sorry for you. Actually, I haven't felt better in years." I appreciated her concern for my feelings, but I'm not sure that I needed the sympathy; I was just pleased to see that she was so strong. In time, we were *both* better and looked forward to remaining healthy for a long time to come.

I don't think that I can fully describe my feelings for my daughter. Every time I see her I feel a special relationship, a closeness that comes only from a shared experience and sacrifice. I don't think of her as having my kidney. It's hers. The joy that she brings our family, and the vital work that she is performing in her own young family is worth all the unpleasantness that I may have experienced. It's definitely worth that small part of my body that gives her life. With any luck it should continue to function in her for years, and with the help of the Lord she should be able to live a full and rewarding life as a mother and wife. These are blessings that are worth any amount of sacrifice.

I have tried to remember the great kindness of the Primary Children's Hospital. I'll never forget their concern for me and my family, the nurses who treated us as if we were their best friends. Some years ago I instituted the Senators' Ski Cup, in which senators from around the country come to Utah every year to participate in a ski competition. Several corporate sponsors also participate, and all the net proceeds are donated to the Primary Children's Hospital for charitable care. Over the years, this has amounted to over a million dollars going toward the hospital's great work. Many of my colleagues have been so impressed with the hospital that they have made additional personal contributions. The Primary Children's Hospital still gives treatment to all children, regardless of their family's ability to pay. This is indeed a Christian service, and in light of the trials facing today's world, it is a gift of hope—and sometimes of life—to those who receive its service.

Over the years I have noticed that adversity has been the springboard to many of my tenderest moments. It has brought me closer to my family and to God. Through these experiences, through the pain and sorrow of loss, through illness and accident, I have learned that there are really very few things of ultimate importance in this life. The things of this world, the things that we can obtain with money and power, are almost meaningless compared to the greater responsibilities and joys of creating an eternal family. All the money in the world could not have prevented my first wife's cancer or guaranteed her subsequent healing from it. The fact that I was a senator in the most powerful nation on earth could not alter the fact that my daughter had diabetes. No amount of wealth or influence could reduce the swelling in Jennifer's head when her skull was cracked in a fall. And, most important, no amount of power in this world can guarantee safety for me and my family in the next. That requires the gospel of Jesus Christ. That requires priesthood. That requires personal faith. Through the trying experiences of my life, I have learned that nothing is as important as God and family. Only priesthood power can work the miracles that are needed for both body and spirit. Priesthood power can heal the soul; it can repair the damaged body and restore a crippled spirit. It can be the source of greater happiness than all the power and money in the world. Operating correctly in a worthy priesthood holder, it can bring eternities of joy. I know that through the priesthood I have tasted a portion of this joy, and I hope I will be worthy to enjoy its ultimate fullness in the world to come. As I come closer to my family, I realize that I am coming closer to the Lord. As I look at my children now, and remember the priesthood blessings I have given them, I know that my entire family has been blessed by each blessing they received. We were all made stronger, regardless of who received the actual blessing. We have all been blessed, and together as a family, I look forward to an eternity of perfect joy.

I may be a skeptic as a senator, but as a priesthood holder and father I'm a believer.

. . . In God

There is one supreme fact in the universe. It eclipses all other truths, all thought, all being, all emotion.

God lives.

I know he lives as I know that I am alive. This simple fact has meant more to me than all else I know. Because of it I am able to live with hope, joy, and peace. Nothing else can give me this security. No amount of money or influence can grant me this peace. I know that I will meet my first wife, Hazel, on the other side of the veil. I *know* this. I know that my entire family, Kathleen and all my children and grandchildren, will meet there, and if we are worthy, we will continue as a family forever. I know that God the Father and his Son, Jesus Christ, love me. I have felt their love and know it extends to each person on earth. I know that they are concerned for me, that they work, in ways I cannot comprehend, for my joy and for the joy of each person on earth.

I wasn't born with this knowledge. Like all people who have received testimonies of the existence of God, I have had to work for it and try to live worthy of it. As I matured, the knowledge came, a little at a time, until somewhere along the way my faith in it became firm. Of course, there were moments when I was more sure than at other times, but I don't think I ever doubted. I have always wanted to believe, and perhaps that has been the key to my gaining a knowledge of God.

Like most Utah boys, I was raised in the Church and attended all my meetings—Sunday School, priesthood, sacrament meeting on Sundays, and Primary on Tuesdays. And living the standards of the Church has been a way of life for me for as far back as I can remember. I served in Aaronic Priesthood quorum presidencies, got my hundred percent stickers, participated in road shows, ward parties, dances, and even performed once or twice before the ward, not without embarrassment, though. Once when I was eight, I was asked to play "America" on the piano before the ward. I had been taking piano lessons for a while, and somebody must have figured that I knew what I was doing. Well, I didn't. I had to memorize that song, note for note, until it was ingrained in my head. The day finally came when I was in the chapel before the whole ward. I'll never forget how it looked from that vantage point, and I'll never forget how scared I got. I froze. I didn't play a single note. I sat in front of the piano and couldn't figure out what I was supposed to do. Finally my Primary teacher came up and said, "Thank you, Jake. We appreciate your effort, and we'll have to ask you to perform for us again sometime." Of course they never did. And I never wanted them to. I can still sit down and play "America," blindfolded, but *then* I couldn't remember it for my life.

Even when I was older I had uneasy moments. I was nineteen and had just been ordained an Elder. Joseph B. Wirthlin was our bishop. He's an Apostle now. For some reason, he had the faith in me to call me to be the Aaronic Priesthood General Secretary for our ward. That's a position we don't have anymore, but then it was considered quite a responsible calling. A week or so after I was set apart, I attended my first Stake General Secretary's Meeting, in the Bonneville Stake. I walked into the room where I had been instructed to go, and I saw a bunch of older men. I saw Judge Jeppeson, who was a Juvenile Court Judge, LeGrande Backman, a prominent attorney, and several other important men, most of them in their forties or fifties. (That was old to me then; now it hardly qualifies as experienced.) I turned around and walked out. I knew I didn't belong where those men were, so I went down the hall looking for the right meeting. I asked somebody in the hallway if he knew where the General Secretary's Meeting was, and he said, "Sure, right back where you came from." So I turned around and went back in the room and sat down. The meeting hadn't started yet, and it wasn't long before one of the men asked me if I had the right room. I looked at him and said, "This is the General Secretary's Meeting, isn't it?"

"Yes."

"Well, I'm the new General Secretary in our ward."

I can still remember the eyes of some of the men growing wider, then hearing whispers about Bishop Wirthlin—"Why in the world would he pick such a boy?"

But that was the beginning of a great relationship between me and my bishop. I didn't go on a mission because we were in the Korean War then, and the Government only allowed one missionary per ward to serve full-time. (As it turned out, I only had the option of either enlisting in the service or being drafted into the service; so I eventually enlisted.) But before that it was wonderful working side by side with a leader like Bishop Wirthlin. He made me feel like I could do whatever the Lord wanted me to do, and, even though I may not have had the testimony I would later develop, he made me want to serve in the Church. I would have to say that Bishop Wirthlin had more influence over my life than any other man except my father. His trust in me made a huge difference in my view of myself. Because of his trust, which I always tried to live up to, my self-confidence grew a great deal. Those men may not have understood my bishop's logic in calling a young kid like myself to that position, but I never saw Bishop Wirthlin vacillate once in the decision. He supported me completely.

After a year of service in this calling I had my first experience with real testimony—when I *knew* that the Lord lived. It came on my first cruise with the Navy. I was still an undergraduate at the University of Utah but had enlisted and was required to serve a two-month cruise with other midshipmen, both from the Naval Academy and other universities. This was training for us as we worked toward our commissions at school.

I was twenty years old and had never been away from home for more than a day or two. Now I was on a World War II Fletcher-Class destroyer, the USS Ross, DD563, departing from Norfolk, Virginia, for Edinburgh, Scotland. I might as well have been a million miles away from Salt Lake City right then. I suddenly found myself in a world of strangers and severe physical inconvenience. As we pulled into the open sea, I could tell right away that it wasn't going to be an enjoyable trip. The ship was only about thirty-five feet wide and was over three hundred feet long, which meant that it rolled a lot. If there was a wave, we felt it. The weather got considerably colder as we headed north, and the winds increased to gales. I'll never forget the green and blue water crashing over our bow and washing down our decks—so much so that the crew was soon confined to quarters. We couldn't go above deck because of the danger of the high seas, and we couldn't move much below deck because of the closed spaces.

Everybody got seasick. We were wedged in quarters so small that we had to stay on our bunks, which were stacked five high. There was so little room between each bunk that you had to get out of bed to turn over. We literally couldn't turn from our stomachs onto our backs and stay in bed. Because of this, everybody started throwing up over the sides of their bunks instead of going to the bathroom. In no time at all, we were awash in vomit, and the smell itself was enough to make us sick, even if the seasickness didn't. I looked over once and saw a guy on the second bunk lean out and throw up on the floor. Another man on the fifth bunk, right above him, leaned out at the same time and threw up on the back of his head. That was about the only comic relief we got the whole way. I remember thinking that this cruise was punishment for something I had done in my life. Every minute I was awake I was thinking of ways to desert when I got to Scotland. It was a recurring thought: *I'm going to desert. I can't take this. I'm never coming back.* And it got to the point where I couldn't stand being there anymore. I started to cry. I wanted to talk to my mother; I wanted to go back to Salt Lake; I was the only member of the Church on the ship, and I wanted to go back home where my friends were. I didn't see how I was going to make it the whole way.

For the first time in my life, I didn't have anybody to turn to except the Lord. I had always prayed, but I had never felt such a need for the Lord before. Now I began to pray with everything I had, with my whole heart. I asked him to be with me, to give me peace, to help me through this. I didn't say it out loud, and I certainly didn't kneel, but I closed my eyes and gave the most heart-felt prayers of my life. I didn't see a light. I didn't have any inspiration or revelations, but soon a calmness came into me. I began to feel a pervasive peace that seemed to distance me somehow from the situation around me. The ship didn't stop rolling, and I didn't stop throwing up, but the panic completely left me, and I was as calm and reassured as I ever had been at home. I knew the Lord was gracing me with his spirit. I had never felt it like that before, but I knew, absolutely, what was happening. During a three or four day period, when the weather was the worst and the men were the sickest, I felt the greatest peace. And I knew at that time that I could make it. From that point on, I felt stronger, and surer, and by the time we got to Edinburgh I had no desire at all to desert.

That was when I really discovered the Lord. It was also when I really discovered prayer. Coming from a sheltered home in the valleys of Utah, I had never needed to find the Lord for myself. But when I truly needed him, he came.

We stopped for a time in London, and I went immediately to Hyde Park Chapel to be with the Saints. After an experience like that, I never wanted to be apart from the members of the Church again. As I attended their meetings, I was gratified to see that the British Saints were almost identical to the Saints I had always known. They preached the same gospel, blessed and partook of the sacrament, and bore testimonies of the truthfulness of the

Church. After sacrament meeting, these kind people introduced themselves to me and some offered to take me home to dinner. I accepted an invitation and found myself in a Latter-day Saint home almost no different than that of my own. The Spirit of the Lord was there, and for the first time in my life I really understood what the companionship of the Spirit was. I knew at that point, *for myself,* that the gospel was true and that God literally did love us.

We boarded the ship again, and I felt that companionship with me still. I never got seasick again. I never found myself feeling lonely or despairing. I never entertained thoughts of desertion again during my entire stay in the Service. Once I found the Lord for myself, I was ready to serve in any capacity needed of me and perform almost any sacrifice.

After leaving Edinburgh, our ship went north to Oslo, Norway, and we were able to spend a few days there. My great grandmother Uvaas had been born in the little town of Burseskong, in the 1830s. She had joined the Church when she was nineteen and was immediately kicked out of her home. Her parents told her to leave and never come back. She went to America for the rest of her life, settling in Fairview, Utah. Now in 1953, a full century since she had been exiled from her home, I was in Norway, not too far from her little town. I caught a train for Trondheim, where the mission home was, and spoke with the mission president. I asked if a couple of missionaries could go up to Burseskong with me to visit my great grandmother's family. I had an uncle years before who went to this part of Norway on his mission and met some of his grandmother's family. They had showed no interest in the Church then but were kind to him and asked about his grandmother Uvaas. The president and the elders had never heard of this town. They had missionaries all over the country, but they had never come across this town. We got the encyclopedia out and found that the name of "Burseskong" had been changed to Skaun and that it wasn't too far away. The president was glad to let a couple of elders travel with me, hopefully to meet some of this family. Actually, I only knew one family member's name, Ingemar Uvaas, and he would have been very elderly by then if he were still alive.

When the elders realized that I didn't know the people that we were going to look up, and that I only remembered one name, they shook their heads and made passing comments about needles in haystacks. They also recognized the area as a difficult tracting area; the people had never been receptive to the gospel there. Before we left, we said a prayer, and I remember bowing my head and asking the Lord to direct us in finding my relatives.

We traveled on a large bus for some time then sat in small kiosk and waited for another bus to take us the rest of the way. When we got on the new bus, I felt impressed to ask the missionaries, who spoke Norwegian, to ask the bus driver if he knew anything about the area around Skaun. They asked him, and he replied that he knew it quite well, that he was from there. Then the missionaries pointed at me and said that I was looking for a relative there, somebody named Ingemar Uvaas. He turned to them and said, "That's me."

The missionaries got excited, as they sometimes do when they think great things are about to happen. Ingemar looked back and we just stared at each other a moment, and then we starting talking, the missionaries translating for us. By the time we got to Skaun, I had learned that this wasn't the actual Ingemar Uvaas I had been looking for; he was dead. This was his son. He took me and the elders to his home and told us all he knew about my great grandmother, and he knew quite a lot. He told us the whole story about how she had been kicked out of her home and how, at the age of nineteen, she had walked down the road and never come back. He took us up to her old house, the one she had been born in, then showed us the road that she had walked down. The setting was spectacular; the house sits on a hill overlooking a lake at the bottom of a beautiful valley. I imagined the heart-ache of this young woman as she trudged down the road, knowing that she may not see her family or friends or this beautiful valley again. The image of this moment, seeing that lake, her town, and that valley for the last time, must of stayed with her the rest of her life—as it has with me. She knew the gospel was true, and no amount of sacrifice was too great to remain true to it.

Ingemar and I separated that day as more than good friends. There was a bond that developed that has since led to our families coming close and visiting each other. The missionaries might have been disappointed, I suppose, because little progress was made in sharing the gospel with Ingemar and his family. But simply reestablishing the family ties seemed more important at this time. Later, I had a cousin, Jan Christensen, who served a mission in that part of Norway, and he too became good friends with the family there. This led to a visit by one of our distant cousins to the United States. She lived with my mother while she attended the University of Utah. She, too, did not join the

Church, but more important bonds were made, bonds that may be of great worth at a later date, perhaps in a different world.

After this cruise, I realized that in a certain way members of the Church living outside Utah have a greater appreciation for the gospel than many of us here. I could see how living without the constant influence of the Church could help you to find your own relationship with Christ in a more direct way. When you find yourself alone as a member of the Church, and there's just you and the Lord, you develop a much closer relationship with him. Because of this, I envy people living away from the center of the Church. I know that they've got an advantage in some ways in living the true spirit of the gospel.

Scriptures

Several years before this cruise, on my twelfth birthday, I was given a Triple Combination by some friends of our family. It is one of my most prized possessions. When not using it, I have kept it in the same box it came in, and after forty-eight years the book is still beautiful. On the cruise, I was afraid that it would be damaged by sea water, but it somehow stayed dry. Over the years since, I have kept special letters and documents in the box along with the book, letters from my father and mother, my patriarchal blessing, and personal papers. When I pick it up now, I feel like Joseph Smith must have when he picked up the Golden Plates for the first time. It is sacred to me, and I open it with reverence and read from the book's pages with a special feeling. Although I had owned the book for several years, it was after my experience with the Spirit aboard ship that I began to discover the bounty in its pages. I began from that time to fall in love with its teachings. Just as I had discovered the power of prayer in the ship, I now began to discover the power of the scriptures.

As I began to read the Book of Mormon and Doctrine and Covenants with new intent, I found that the Lord spoke to me through their words. I began finding answers to my problems and questions. I found that ideas came into my mind helping me make better decisions. I found that the scriptures are *very* practical. Their teachings give us guidance that, when coupled with the Spirit, apply specifically to our lives. The Lord speaks to us this way, using our hearts and our minds in conjunction with the scriptures to give us new insights. This miraculous power of the scriptures still stirs me today. Often when wrestling with a difficult problem, I will find the answer in a passage of scripture. A verse that has often given me strength is Matthew 17:20: " . . . for verily I say unto you, if ye have faith as a mustard seed, ye shall say unto this mountain, Remove hence to yonder place; and it shall remove; and nothing shall be impossible unto you." The knowledge that "nothing shall be impossible" to one with faith has encouraged me many times when I thought I was fighting insurmountable odds.

My favorite book of scripture is the New Testament.

It was in the New Testament that Joseph Smith found the inspiration to pray—again, the Lord speaking to somebody through the scriptures. It is in the New Testament where we learn of the life and mission of Jesus Christ. It is a book of love, and although it describes the cruelty of certain people in persecuting and finally crucifying the Savior, it is ultimately a book of kindness and peace. The Lord's teachings of turning the other cheek, of forgiving your enemies, of treating others as you would have them treat you, touch me in such a way as to make me want to employ this same love and forgiveness in my own life. I find great comfort in the New Testament, and I probably find more answers to my questions there than anywhere else. The injunction, for example, in Matthew 7:7-8 to "Ask, and it shall be given you; seek, and ye shall find . . ." has often prodded me to kneel and ask the Lord for special guidance in a difficult moment.

The life of the Savior is miraculous to me. Having served in circles with some of the greatest leaders in the world, I can see the vast difference between them and the carpenter's son from Galilee. I have served with the wisest men in global politics, and none of them have wisdom that compares with the Savior's. The Beatitudes alone set the Savior apart from all the philosophers and leaders of the world. His teachings were radical at the time, and they were seen as subordinating the laws of Moses. But when practiced, they led people to a higher, more exalted level of life. He himself *lived* these teachings, and in this aspect alone he is distinguished from all other leaders before and after him. I am often reminded of the reaction of the people to Jesus when he first began teaching them with power:

> And when the sabbath day was come, he began to teach in the synagogue: and many hearing him were astonished, saying, From whence hath this man these things? and what wisdom is this which is given unto him, that even such mighty works are wrought by his hands? (Mark 6:2.)

Not only was his wisdom great, but he personified his teachings, *showing* us the way to purer living, thus becoming the goal himself for us to strive for. Because the New Testament shows me the life of the Lord, as well as his teachings, it is for me the most immediate, the most powerful book on earth.

The Savior's atonement and resurrection stand as the greatest miracles of mankind. I believe that he literally did atone for our sins and rise from the dead, and in so conquering death he blessed all mankind with the promise of resurrection—of living forever in the body. Because of that, I consider Easter our most sacred holiday. I love Christmas as a time for families to gather and celebrate the birth of Christ, but I find in Easter the greater celebration of hope and wonder. I stand in awe of his atonement for our sins, of his love for *all* people, of his power over death and the gift of eternal life he is able to offer. He was at once the most humane and the most divine of Adam's children. He incorporated all the heights and depths of existence in a life of complete peace.

A couple of years ago Kathleen and I were in Jerusalem during Easter. On Palm Sunday we joined the procession from the Mount of Olives down the hill, through the Kidron Valley, and into the gates of the old city. We experienced the walk much as He and the Apostles must have experienced it, and a special spirit came to us. We went to the Garden Tomb and saw the place where he may have lain for three days. Again, we felt a beautiful peace there, a feeling that seemed to whisper that the Savior had been there. We were taken by David Galbraith, the BYU Jerusalem Center's director, into an underground prison, a place where the Savior may have been held. Roman writings are still on the walls there, and as you walk on those stones and contemplate that the Savior may have walked on those same stones, you sense an awe come over you, a spirit, again, that whispers sacredness. The area that touched me most deeply was the Sea of Galilee, especially the northern part, where it is still rural. In Jerusalem, the places you see are all several feet above the actual ground that the Savior walked on. All the paths he trod and homes he stayed in are covered by two thousand years of dust. The Sea of Galilee, though, is still the same, with the beaches and surrounding areas virtually identical to when he was there. I was in tears most of the time as I walked on the ground where he is said to have delivered the Beatitudes. It didn't matter if I was on the exact ground or if we were a half mile away, what mattered was the spirit present there. I took a small boat out into the Sea of Galilee and stood up in it and looked out over the water, visualizing the Savior walking across it to the far shore. I felt the Spirit and wept. He did walk across it. He did do all the miracles and teach all the truths that the New Testament says he did. Two thousand years later it's almost as if he is still there, still speaking words of truth and life.

My testimony of him is that he lives. He is the Savior of all mankind, of those who believe and of those who refuse to believe. All knees will bow and every tongue confess. This testimony has been a strength to me not only in my personal life but in my professional life as well.

Prayer

Although I believe that there are inappropriate times to invoke the power or name of the Lord, I also believe that there are many more times when it is not only appropriate but necessary. I would never dream of asking the Lord to help me win a game, for example, or kneel in an end zone and publicly thank him for the touchdown he had just caused me to make, but I would, and often have, bowed my head in silent prayer and asked for wisdom or strength in difficult circumstances. Sometimes I simply ask for the peace necessary for my mind to function at its best capacity. Usually, instead of receiving specific answers to questions I am working on, I receive that peace, and then I am able to conquer what had before seemed insurmountable. During the administration of President Jimmy Carter, for example, I became an early and outspoken opponent of one of his chief policies. He had just signed the Salt II agreement with the Soviet Union, regarding the control of nuclear arms, and he wanted the Senate to sign it. Although I am not opposed to the control of nuclear arms, I *was* opposed to the particular way in which this agreement tried to do it. I felt that it restricted us in unfair and ultimately unwise ways. Because of my stance, I was often asked to speak on talk shows like "Meet the Press," and at other venues. I had lost my nervousness about appearing on television a long time before, but an invitation was given in which I would participate in a debate with Iowa Senator, John Culver, on national TV. The debate would be aired live across the nation at prime time, assuring an audience of millions.

Here, I had the responsibility of representing my side of the debate, which was shared by many in the Congress, and to do it with an opponent like Senator John Culver and with questioners like Averil Herriman. These were some of the finest talents in the world, and they wanted to pick my position apart. The debate was to be held in the Kennedy Center with a large and prominent audience.

Before the debate, I sat in the car in the Kennedy Center parking lot and bowed my head. I told Heavenly Father that I knew the issues, that I had studied them to the best of my ability and had my opinions concerning them. I didn't ask him to give me any special insights or powers of speech, I just asked him to bless me with peace that my mind might be clear. As I finished the prayer, I remember a sweetness coming over me, a calm that filled my whole body. I knew at that time that I would be all right. I knew that I could handle the questions and the pressure of a live, national audience. As I walked in and took my place on the stage, that feeling of peace and confidence stayed with me. I don't remember everything that I said that night, though I suppose it is recorded and I could find out, but I remember thinking that all was going well, that I was explaining the issues concisely and articulately and that others were understanding them. I didn't look at the debate as something I had to win, but rather as a forum to express important ideas and facts to the American people. The success I enjoyed in doing this was directly attributable to the spirit of peace that I possessed. I felt that the Lord blessed me, through his peace, to do my best.

Other times arise, of course, when you need specific answers to pressing dilemmas. Sometimes, however, no answer seems to be available. No matter how much you pray or how much you ponder, nothing seems to come. But I have learned that often we look for a dramatic answer, almost like a billboard lighting up, when in reality what we receive is a soft whisper of peace. And that answer can take weeks or months, or sometimes years, to receive. Then, too, you might be trying to make a major decision and simply forget to ask the Lord for help. As much as I believe in prayer, I still find myself doing this sometimes.

In the last several months I have had to make a decision as to whether I would run for reelection to the Senate. I had already served nearly eighteen years and knew that I would probably win a fourth term if I ran. I had won my last two elections with over seventy percent of the vote, and there was no reason to think that this campaign would be any different. Something inside me, though, questioned the wisdom of running again. I thought about it for weeks, debating it in my mind, then began gradually agonizing over it. I was spending most of my time in Washington of course, and I began calling Kathleen back in Utah nearly every night, asking her what she thought I should do. On weekends I was just as relenting, discussing the pros and cons with her for hours. This went on for months. Finally, one night she said, "Honey, I don't care what you do. I just can't keep spending every night on the phone with you. Have you talked to the Lord yet?" I hung up and the thought hit me: "I can't believe it, I haven't prayed about it."

I was stunned. I had gone all these months agonizing over a decision as important as this, driving my wife crazy, going through all the "T" formulas and using every other kind of stratagy I could think of, and I hadn't approached the Lord about it. I knelt that night and asked for his help.

An answer didn't come right away, but the anxiety immediately left. For the next month or so before making the decision, I was free of torment and uncertainty. I knew that when I did make the decision it would be the right one. Finally, when the decision came, I knew that it was what I was searching for; I knew that I was to come home from the Senate and be with my family. The answer was peaceful and strong. Interestingly enough, soon after I announced my decision, I received a phone call and was offered a job for quite a large amount of money when I retired from the Senate. The job would have been interesting and challenging, but I asked if it would allow me to remain with my family in Utah. The other party said no; it would require me to be on the East Coast. I said I wasn't interested. He said, "What's the matter, isn't the money enough?" And I said, "The money's more than enough; it's more than I ever dreamed of making, but I belong at home." The answer had been plain to me, not only was I to retire from the Senate, but I was to spend more time at home, and Utah is my home.

Patriarchal Blessing

My patriarchal blessing has had a powerful and sustaining influence on my testimony. I received it when I was nineteen but then put it away and didn't find it again until I was about thirty-five years old. I know that we are encouraged to read our patriarchal blessings often and prayerfully to help give our lives direction, but after going in the Navy I lost track of it. If I had been asked at that time to list what it said to me, I couldn't have done it. I found it, though, when I was thirty-five and was already serving as City Commissioner, in Salt Lake. It had been given to me by Eldred G. Smith, the Church Patriarch, and although he hadn't known me personally, he seemed to see into the depths of my soul, telling me what faults to beware of, what strengths to work on, and most amazingly, what type of mission the Lord had planned for me.

As I read through the blessing again, some sixteen years after receiving it, I was startled to see that it emphasized a "special mission" of service that the Lord had given me "at the time of my birth." Then, in five different sections of the blessing it exhorted me to use my abilities "in the service of my fellowman." I was humbled by the prophetic power of the blessing, by the admonitions to use my "talents and abilities in service unto [my] fellowmen," and by the many promises which were then given. Having already embarked on a path of public service, a path which I had not considered at all at the time of this blessing, I was amazed at the clearness of the direction. I have since found great comfort and further direction in reading its words. I know that the Lord spoke through his chosen servant in giving me this counsel. I know that it was literally given from a Father to a son.

Example

The old saying in the Church is that you never know who might be watching you. I was attending a function at the Hyatt Regency in Washington, DC, recently, and was sitting at the head table. The head waiter approached me and offered me a diet A&W Root Beer. Others had been brought coffee, tea, or alcohol. I thanked the waiter for his consideration and asked him how he knew, and he said, "Well, I heard that you were a Mormon and that you didn't believe in drinking those other things, so I thought you'd like a root beer." He was right, but I had no idea that he knew. I wonder how many others over the years have been watching me as a Mormon first and a senator second. I hope that I have lived my life such that they have not been disappointed.

Sometimes I have even been aware of people watching me and listening to me as a member of the Church, and I still didn't know how I affected them. I was invited to speak at a multi-stake meeting in Atlanta, Georgia, some years ago. I don't even remember what I spoke about, but after the meeting a fellow came up to me and said, "Senator, thank you." He had tears in his eyes, and I said, "for what?" He said, "After hearing you tonight, I'm going to join the Church." I was surprised. Certainly I hadn't said anything that would convert somebody to the Church. The Regional Representative there, my good friend, Dick Winder, overheard the conversation and gave the man a hug and congratulated him. After the fellow had left, I asked Dick about his story. He said that the man had been investigating the Church for years and that the missionaries had joked about him being their prime investigator. He went to all the meetings; in fact he was one of the most active members (or nonmembers) in the ward, but he never wanted to make the commitment of baptism. Now, because of my talk, supposedly, he wanted to join the Church. Of course, it wasn't anything I said that made the change. He simply felt the Spirit, and the Spirit told him what to do, but somehow my being there did what no set of missionaries could accomplish. It was a very humbling thought, and it made me want to be worthy of the Spirit every time I spoke in the future.

You never know who you might touch. On other occasions I have spoken at missionary conferences, often near Washington where another friend of mine, Jon Huntsman, was a mission president. Nonmembers were invited to attend, and, again, some expressed a change afterwards, a willingness to receive baptism and membership in the Church. I know that I didn't convince them that the gospel was true, but I did try to be worthy of the

Spirit, and the Spirit touched them. Once, a nonmember gentleman came up to me after a talk and asked if he could visit with me further. He was bitter about not being able to attend his daughter's wedding in the temple. We talked for hours, and we later corresponded for some time. No matter what I told him, though, he would not be reconciled to the Church. He never did accept the gospel that I know of. Again, *we* can't convert anybody. Only the Spirit can do that, and the Spirit will only touch those who are ready for it. We can be worthy of the Spirit, but we can't force others to receive it.

Perhaps the most powerful missionary experience I ever had came without my knowing it. A lady journalist asked me if she could interview me for a Christian magazine. I was delighted of course and spent quite a long time with her, over two or three interviews. These were probably the most in-depth interviews I had ever had, and when they were over she knew just about everything that I knew about Jake Garn and the Church of Jesus Christ of Latter-day Saints. She specifically wanted to know what I, as a person, felt about God, Christ, and Bible teachings. She didn't want me repeating Church doctrine—just my own beliefs. And that's just what she got. When we were through, though, she realized that the two were just about identical. I didn't hear from her for months, but I didn't forget her frankness and persistent questioning. Then, about six months later, she sent me a letter in which she thanked me for teaching her the gospel and said that she had joined the Church. I was shocked. I called her immediately, both to express congratulations and to ask what happened, and she told me that the interviews had lit a spark of curiosity in her. She didn't know that a politician could have such strong feelings about morality and honesty and the gospel of Jesus Christ. After finishing our interviews, she had called the missionaries and asked for the missionary lessons. She was ready. She was prepared for the gospel, she just didn't know it. And what's more, I didn't know it. Again, I learned that same lesson—you never know who you'll touch. You'll never know who's prepared—until you have shared your testimony.

Three Influences

For most of my adult life I've had three influences in most of the decisions I've made. They come to me in this order: my knowledge of the Savior, the influence of my parents, and prayer. No matter how difficult the decisions in my life have been, the combination of these three influences have always solved them. I have already shared my feelings on the life of the Savior and my testimony of his love for me. And I have shared sacred experiences with prayer. The influences of my mother and father, however, are more difficult to share. My mother has been dead for a number of years now, but her words and expressions still come back to me. I'll never forget her teachings about generosity or the value of kindness. I'll never forget her keen sense of humor and how she could make a gathering bright just by her presence. She was something of a legend in our neighborhood. She knew every postman and milkman we had by name. She knew the owners of the local businesses and the names of every child and parent in our neighborhood. She was one of the most forgiving people I have ever known and one of the most charitable. As I matured I realized that I was blessed with a near perfect mother. Just before I left on the cruise mentioned earlier, my mother handed me the following letter. Nearly forty years later it still makes me emotional.

Wed. July 8, 1953
My dear son:

This is your last night home before you leave for your cruise, and I want to write a few lines to carry with you on this, your first long trip away from home. Something you can read when you are lonely, as I am sure you will be at times. It will bring us close together as we shall always be, no matter how many miles between us.

I wish I could tell you how much I love you, how very dear you are to me. Dearer than life itself. Those I love I want to protect, almost unwisely, so it has been well for you that you have had Dad's good practical advice and guidance.

Your going away on this first great adventure has come at a time when I can give you so little materially, but I give you my love and devotion, and my faith in you. [I am] confident that you will live as you have in the past, clean and fine, never losing that belief you have in your religion and its rewards.

You are going to meet many different people, son, fine splendid men who will become very good friends even though their ideas and interpretation of life may differ greatly from yours. Remember kind, quiet words are far more effective than argumentative, harsh ones. Be tolerant. That doesn't mean you have to compromise with your high ideals. Just respect other people's views; it doesn't mean you have to accept them.

The little weaknesses in your character can be overcome and your good qualities enhanced in proportion to your desires and ability to self-improve.

This is your first big test, to live with a group of men, earn their respect and affection; give that same respect and affection in return. You have a wonderful personality. Use it and learn to love people sincerely. Life is easier when you do. I know I have endowed you with an understanding heart. Cultivate it. I want you to have those qualities more than worldly goods.

You are inherently generous. Generosity doesn't always mean with the pocketbook.

I have watched you in the last year overcome little faults that were harmful; develop those attributes that will make you a happy man. These aren't just pretty words. I speak from experience. Don't be irritated by other people; they have a right to their opinions. Our silence doesn't mean our acceptance.

I shall miss you every minute of the day and night, waiting for the sound of your car. [I shall miss you] early in the morning when it's so beautiful, and I have no tuna sandwiches to make, and at that time of day when we would draw each other's attention to the sunset over Great Salt Lake. It's a beautiful world, son. Live so you can enjoy it and be free to enjoy it.

My prayers shall be with you constantly, Dear. Don't forget to say yours. Sometime we are working or serving under conditions that makes it hard to kneel, but remember our song, "Prayer is the soul's sincere desire, uttered or unexpressed."

Take care of yourself and remember, I am with you even though far away,

Mother.

My mother was the true matriarch of our family—and not just of my immediate family, of the whole family. She was like the honey that attracts the honeybees, and her home was the hive. We enjoyed almost constant visits from extended family members. I remember once, long after I was married, coming into her kitchen one morning and finding two of the scroungiest looking teenagers I had ever seen sitting down at her table and having breakfast. I was quiet until they left, then I said, "Mother, where did you dig up those two?" "Oh," she said, "they knocked on the door this morning and said that they knew my grandson and that he had told them to stop in if they were ever hungry. I couldn't turn them away, now, could I?"

As I mature, I realize that in many ways she was the personification of Christlikeness in my life. She showed me how to be like the Savior, how to live so that people will want to like me and trust me. Today, when I have to make a difficult choice, I often ask myself, "What would my mother do?" Perhaps because I can visualize her so well, or because I remember her sweet spirit and wisdom, I hear the answers coming from her. I can see what she would do, and in every case it turns out to be right. When she helped me understand the problems I was causing with my son, for example, when he needed my love and patience more than my criticism, she gave me guidance that would last for all of my children. When she helped me through the terrible ordeal of my first wife's death, she gave me a promise that still remains with me, that if I would obey the commandments of the Lord I would find happiness in this life and have a strong family. Her influence will undoubtedly remain with me forever.

My father died of cancer in 1971, right in the middle of my campaign for mayor. He was a civil engineer and built many roads throughout Utah as well as most of the early airports. Dad was a great compliment to my mother's love and kindliness as he was immovably practical and down-to-earth. He was the best example of what honesty and integrity are that I have ever known.

When I was in my teens my father purchased ten building lots in the south part of Salt Lake County. He subrogated them to a builder who built ten homes on them, sold two or three, then went bankrupt. My father had the choice of taking the properties back, which still had a large debt against them, or let the bank repossess them. Because he felt so strong about paying back his obligations, he refused to let the bank repossess the properties. For the next few years our family struggled a great deal financially as he made payments every month. Periodically he sold one or two, which lowered the amount we owed. Finally we had only one home for sale, but it had not attracted any attention for months. One Saturday morning while I was mowing our front lawn, my father came running down the porch steps and said, "Jake! Jake, I have sold the last home. We're out of it!"

"Did you get a good deal?" I asked.

"No, but it doesn't make any difference. There are no more payments." He was happier than I had seen him in a long time.

About a half hour later a young real estate agent drove up, and he had a standard real estate contract in his hand. My father met him by his car and began talking to him. As I continued mowing, I noticed their conversation getting louder and a little heated. I walked over to them and said, "What's the matter, Dad?"

"I'll tell you what's the matter," the real estate agent said. "I've got another offer for that house your father is selling, for *six thousand dollars more* than your father has made a verbal agreement for, and he won't sell me the house. He isn't *bound* to keep that agreement. There isn't any court in the land that would make him keep it, and I've got a thousand dollars earnest money right here!"

"Young man," my father said sternly. "You don't understand. *I gave my word.* I would love to sell you that house for your price, and if the other real estate agent is not here by ten A.M. Monday morning with a signed agreement and a check for the earnest money like he promised, then I'll be happy to work with you. But if he *does* show up with those things, then I'm bound—I gave my word."

At that time, six thousand dollars was worth half of my father's annual pay. It would be worth tens of thousands of dollars today, but that didn't dissuade him. On Monday morning the other real estate agent came by with the signed contract and check for the agreed-upon amount, and my father sold him the house. He didn't worry about the six thousand dollars he might have had; he only worried about keeping his commitment. The other real estate agent lost a commission, and my father lost some profits he might have had, but his honor was not something he sold. Integrity was absolutely everything to him. What he taught me then and throughout his life about integrity has been invaluable during my public career. He knew no gray areas. One was either honest or one was dishonest; there was no in between. I'll never forget the advice he had given me on my twelfth birthday. He was in California on a business trip and couldn't be home, so he sent me a letter. It has become one of the most precious documents I own—one I keep in that special little box with my Triple Combination.

10-8-1944

My dear son:

It is just a few days now until Oct. 12, and that will be your 12th birthday. I wish so much that I could spend it with you. My mind goes back 12 years to the night when you were born down there in Richfield and how glad both Mother and I were when Dr. McQuarrie said it was a fine boy, for we had been wanting a boy so much.

. . .

You are at an age now where you will embark in new activities, being a Deacon, a Scout, and going to the gym. You will meet a lot more people, some older, some your age, some younger. Some of these may have a bad influence on you; shun them. Others will have an ever-lasting influence on you for good; cultivate them. In all your doings, your dealings, your games and what not, be fair, be honest, be a sport. There will be times when you or your team will lose, and it is during those times that you can show how big you are by being a good loser. Be a good mixer and make people like you by being clean in mind and body, by doing little things that help people, by being unselfish, by being good and doing good deeds, by being a Scout. Try hard to overcome your shyness and mix more with people. Make them like you like they like your mother. She has a such a wonderful gift for making people like her.

To make good in this world is not easy. It takes lots of hard work, and it is a long road to success, and the only way I know of to reach the end is to plug away and never swerve until you can at last reach the goal you have seen, and when you have reached that one, then go on farther.

I want you to enjoy life to the fullest. Get all the pleasure out of it you can as you go along. Make other people happy and you will be happy. Work hard, play hard, study hard, and always be fair and honest. Never resort to the petty things in life but always look for the best, for the things that will elevate you. From this you will get happiness.

On your 12th birthday hitch your wagon to a star, set your goal that high and resolve that you will never give up until you have reached it.

Son, I am so proud of you. I am expecting big things of you. I know it will take a lot of time and hard work to accomplish it, to get through college and to be the best in whatever field you choose. That indeed is a big order, but I have so much faith in you that I know you will not let me down. You are blessed with a sound body and a brilliant mind, and there is no end to the heights to which you can soar. Again I say I have put in a big order. I have asked a lot but I am betting on you and betting you will come through with flying colors. You will for me, won't you son? For twelve years we have had you, have raised you, worried about you when you were sick, worried about your welfare, and whether you might get hurt or be in danger, but every minute that we have had you and every minute that we have had the girls has been a source of the greatest happiness to both Mother and I. No greater blessing and no greater happiness can come to us than if we can just have you all as long as we live.

It will be such a pleasure to watch your development and your successes through the years. To have you tell me about them. About all the things you do. Also when you have troubles and problems to listen to them and help you solve them. The greatest joy I can get out of life now is to just be with my family to enjoy them. I do so wish I could be at home with you all at this time, but I want to take this means of saying happy birthday to the finest son a proud Dad ever had.

Lots of love from
Dad

I still get emotional as I read this letter from the greatest teacher and friend I ever had. Over the years, more letters came from him, as I left home for the first time, while I was in the Navy, as I began to serve in public office. I cherish them as I do my patriarchal blessing. What a great balance I had in my parents. The combination of their wisdom and talents has been a blessing all my life.

With my mother's soft, gentle words and my father's honest advice, and the Savior's example, and the ultimate power of prayer, I have never been led wrong. I have not always done the right thing in my life, but I have never been misled by these three influences. When I have taken time to sincerely use them, they have been the source of correct, and sometimes profound, wisdom.

Belief

In our high priests group one Sunday we were discussing the value of the gospel of Jesus Christ. Somebody asked what the rest of us would do if we found out that the Church wasn't true. Some said that they would live differently. Some, perhaps jokingly, said that they hoped they hadn't missed out on the pleasures of life for no reason. But, as usual, I was the one who rocked the boat. I said that if I found out tomorrow that the Church wasn't true and that God didn't live and that there was nothing after death, I wouldn't change a single thing in the way I live. I would continue to live the gospel of Jesus Christ as I understand it because virtue is its own reward. I believe that regardless of religious or eternal consequences, people are happier when they live a moral life, when they're honest and kind and charitable. I believe that if the Ten Commandments were actually followed by the people on earth that we would solve many of the world's problems. Wars would become extinct. Lying and stealing would disappear. Even some devastating illnesses, like AIDS, would quickly become eradicated—or better yet, never have started. The Ten Commandments are pretty basic.

They're not hard to understand; they're just hard to live. That's what gets us in trouble.

If I found out that the Church wasn't true, I wouldn't start drinking and smoking. I don't want to kill myself in a car accident or die of lung cancer. I don't want to lose my family or friends because of disloyalty or dishonesty. I don't want to hurt others. I enjoy the life I have, and I have to give credit to the gospel of Jesus Christ, to the Church of Jesus Christ of Latter-day Saints, to the scriptures, and most of all to the Lord for the help I have received. But I know that the Church *is* true. And I know that God lives, and I know that he is waiting for me to return to him. I know that I can have my family there, and be reunited with my mother and father and other family members. I know that I can visit face to face, perhaps arm in arm, with the Lord and receive his love. I know that greater things await me there than I have ever received here.

As I know that there is one truth which eclipses all others, as I know that there is ultimately only one source of joy, and as I know that all meaning is relegated to this one fact, so I also know that I must share it:

God lives.

With these words, with this testimony, I hope that the world may understand *why I believe.*